Breakout for

Breakthrough

Journey for Prophetic Destiny

ALEMU BEEFTU PhD

Breakout for Breakthrough: Journey for Prophetic Destiny

2019 © Alemu Beeftu

First Printing: 2019
Printed in the USA
Published by Alemu Beeftu, Ph.D.
ISBN: 9781691454358

BREAKOUT FOR BREAKTHROUGH

Endorsements

Breakout for Breakthrough is exactly as it states! Alemu Beeftu writes from his extraordinary testimony of one who was born in a small village to becoming a world-class leader with a doctorate degree.

It is life-changing!

Cindy Jacobs
Co-Founder, General International
Founder, Deborah Company
Apostle, Reformation Prayer Network (RPN)
Apostle, Apostolic Council of Prophetic Elders (ACPE)

Alemu Beeftu's life started in a remote farming village in Ethiopia. A burning desire to learn to read took him to a mission school, where he committed his life to Jesus Christ. This was the humble beginning of Alemu's journey for his prophetic destiny. With a passion to hear and obey God, Alemu received a Bible college degree in Africa, traveled to the United States to earn three university degrees, worked for an international organization training Christian leader, and founded a ministry that brings the nations to life in Christ. I've known Alemu for many years, but I continue to be inspired by how God uses him to impart biblical truth, in wisdom and power, around the world.

Reading Alemu's life story—with blessings and miracles beyond imagining—you may think that Alemu is special. But Alemu is simply a child of the Living God and a man totally committed to following the Holy Spirit's leading on a God-ordained journey. It is a journey available to each of us, if we choose it.

If you desire to serve God with success and impact, this book is a "how-to" book. How to live as a new creation in Christ Jesus. How to commit your way to the God who has a meaningful purpose for your life. How to have eternal, kingdom impact for the glory of God. How to start well, walk straight, and finish well. This book is instructive and inspirational. Prepare to have your heart, mind, and spirit opened to what God desires to do in and through you.

Dutch Sheets
Founder, Dutch Sheets Ministries

Today, Alemu Beeftu is a spiritual luminary. But I knew him best when he was a boy, when he walked miles to our mission school in Ethiopia. He would come carrying his food on his back. One day he asked me for a place to pray and I offered my office. Not long after, I heard a noise coming from my office during the night. Thinking it was a thief, I took my flashlight and approached, only to find Alemu praying his heart out.

I remember when Alemu told me, way back then, that he wanted to go to America to study. I laughed to myself because that is the dream of many. But look at what God has done in Alemu's life — one miracle after another! Today Alemu stands tall as an international servant of God. This amazing story is how God brought this young lad into world prominence. I wept as I read it. I could not put it down, nor will you.

Dr. Howard Brant
Deputy Director for Ethiopia, SIM Mission (presently retired).

Breakout for Breakthrough is a concept that will help anyone better understand God's incredible love for us and His desire that we fulfill the purposes He has ordained for us. Alemu's story is amazing. His journey is both inspiring and challenging as we look at our own obstacles, both behind and before us. God will both pursue us and enable us to be used by Him, as we allow Him. I've walked a close journey with Alemu for over more than 30 years. This is a man that God has used, is using, and will continue to use to impact generations. Read this book and allow God to speak to you as you travel your own journey.

Mark Yeadon
Sr. Vice President, Compassion International

To all who haven't had the privilege of knowing Dr. Alemu Beeftu, I encourage you to get to know him through this book and read what makes him tick. To me, this verse sums up Dr. Beeftu's life: *"The God of heaven Himself will prosper us; therefore, we his servants will arise and build, . . ."* (Nehemiah 2:20 NKJV). This book illustrates the beautiful partnership that an ordinary boy had with an almighty God to accomplish God's extraordinary will on earth. It encourages us not to discount our small beginnings, but to build on them and walk the path that the Holy Spirit lays out for us. The way Dr. Beeftu has interlaced biblical principles and stories of his life makes this a practical book that readers can easily relate to. The faithfulness of God is the overall theme of this book and it has renewed my faith and my resolve for my own journey.

I have seen Alemu and Genet Beeftu take steps of faith like those described in this book. I have stayed at their home many times and Dr. Beeftu's consistency in his early morning devotional time (even after long nights in the midst of conferences) has made me respect him all the more. I consider it an honor to make myself accountable to Dr. Beeftu in my life journey. As it is written, God honors those who honor Him. This book is a testimony that God will do the same in our lives if we honor Him.

Fikre Tesfaye
Assistant Director Insurance Collections
Vanderbilt Health One Hundred Oaks

This book holds profound, yet clear-cut, answers to questions of purpose and destiny. I know no one more qualified to speak to the issue of destiny than my friend Alemu Beeftu. Here he opens the amazing story of his life—a journey from peasant farm boy to pastor, author, professor, evangelist, ministry president, global speaker and leader. It would be a fascinating read even if he only gave us a narrative of that remarkable odyssey. Through twists and turns and ups and downs, we witness God's just-at-the-right-time guidance and provision, demonstrating clearly that the life committed to Him is securely in His hands. But Alemu fills in his testimony with biblical principles, lessons learned, and assurances that God is faithful. Through Alemu's story, you can reflect on your own journey and trust that God has a purpose for your life.

Dr. Wess Stafford
President Emeritus, Compassion International
Author of Too Small to Ignore and Just a Minute

CONTENTS

ALEMU BEEFTU PHD

FOREWORD

In Daniel 9, we see a biblical example of a season of desolation coming to an end, so that a season of prophetic fulfillment could begin. Israel had been in captivity in Babylon for 70 years and was still in bondage when Daniel began reading the prophecies of Jeremiah: "In the first year of his reign I, Daniel, understood by the books the number of the years specified by the word of the LORD through Jeremiah the prophet, that He would accomplish seventy years in the desolations of Jerusalem" (Daniel 9:2 NKJV). As Daniel was reading, he suddenly understood that there was a prophecy given many years before and that *now* was the time for that prophecy to be fulfilled. The 70 years of desolation that Jeremiah had prophesied had been completed, and the time had come to break out of captivity.

God always has *now* times in our lives. Daniel knew that it was time for this word to be fulfilled and for captivity to end. We, like Daniel, also need to come to a place in which we understand God's time sequence. I know that in my own life, when it is time for a season of desolation to end, I want it done and its effects off of me. And once I get out of it, I don't want to turn back. That's the attitude we need to have in moving forward into our prophetic destiny. We need to be in close enough relationship with God that we know when to start into a new sequence and a new cycle of life. We need to know when it is time to cast off our desolation and move into a new season.

Breakout for Breakthrough: Journey for Prophetic Destiny by Dr. Alemu Beeftu, is a key book for this season. I believe that God wants you to break out into a new breakthrough even more than you do. You have a prophetic destiny, and this this book will help you uncover that destiny.

I have learned that prophetic destiny is often tied to the generations of our families. I therefore want to be sure that I somehow complete what God has intended for my bloodline. I need to become successful where there has been failure in my family. I need to overcome the enemy where others in my bloodline have not withstood him. To have prophetic fulfillment in our own lives, we need to allow the Lord to revive the unfulfilled prophetic destiny in our family line and give us a success mentality of completion and fulfillment.

Throughout the Bible, we see examples of God's people making prophetic declarations into their situations in order to see His will come about. Such was the case in Ezekiel 36 and 37. God said to Ezekiel:

> But I had concern for My holy name, which the house of Israel had profaned among the nations wherever they went. Therefore, say to the house of Israel, "Thus says the Lord GOD: 'I do not do this for your sake, O house of Israel, but for My holy name's sake, which you have profaned among the nations wherever you went. And I will sanctify My great name, which has been profaned among the nations, which you have

profaned in their midst; and the nations shall know that I am the LORD,' says the Lord GOD, 'when I am hallowed in you before their eyes. For I will take you from among the nations, gather you out of all countries, and bring you into your own land.

Ezekiel 36:21-24 NKJV

There was a process of scattering that had occurred among God's people. Satan knows how to scatter us and draw us into his process of division and scattering. So, what the Lord told Ezekiel was that even though Israel (signified by the bones in Ezekiel 37) had been scattered, He was going to bring them back together. God then gave Ezekiel an understanding of Israel's prophetic destiny that he was to declare into Earth:

The hand of the LORD came upon me and brought me out in the Spirit of the LORD, and set me down in the midst of the valley, and it was full of bones. Then He caused me to pass by them all around, and behold, there were very many in the open valley, and indeed they were very dry. And He said to me, "Son of man, can these bones live?" So, I answered, "O Lord GOD, You know." Again, He said to me, "Prophesy to these bones, and say to them, 'O dry bones, hear the word of the LORD! Thus says the Lord GOD to these bones: 'Surely, I will cause breath to enter into you, and you shall live. I will put sinews on you and bring flesh upon you, cover you with skin and put breath in you; and you shall live. Then you shall know that I am the Lord.'"

Ezekiel 37:1-6 NKJV

Ezekiel took the words that God gave him and declared them into the desolate situation that had overtaken Judah. When Ezekiel declared God's will, things began to happen. The same is true with us. When we see God's prophetic destiny in our lives and begin to declare it, something will happen. However, we have to release faith before we can see the results with our eyes. Sometimes we look for results without releasing faith, but it simply does not work that way. Faith comes first.

Never forget that declarations have power! You are about to begin an amazing journey in reading *Breakout for Breakthrough!* Here is a prophetic declaration that will help you prepare to unlock the next level of God's prophetic destiny in your life:

I declare that God has a purpose for my life. I receive wisdom and revelation over the hope of my calling. I declare that every strategy of hell that has interrupted God's plan for my life will be exposed. I declare that every hindrance that has stopped me from progressing will be revealed and that I will advance in God's plan for my life. I declare that my faith will be stirred. I declare that new strength will come into my spirit. And I declare that the wilderness will blossom and God's glory will be seen in my life! I declare that the best is yet ahead!

This is your time to breakout!

Dr. Chuck D. Pierce
President, Global Spheres, Inc.
President, Glory of Zion International Ministries

BREAKOUT FOR BREAKTHROUGH

Introduction

Why am I writing this book? Over the many years of ministry, people have asked about my life's journey. As I talk about things that have happened in my life, I look back and give glory to God for the great things that He has done for me personally.

- How did I, who had grown up in remote Ethiopia, a farming community, manage to earn a Ph.D. from Michigan State University, the ninth largest university in the U.S.?
- How did I manage to travel to over 50 nations teaching and preaching the Gospel?
- How was it possible for me to envision the future?

That is just the beginning of the questions. People are amazed! And I am amazed! There are so many miracles that have happened in my life's journey for prophetic destiny. Typically, I give a brief response to satisfy the curious. But I believe now is the time to share some of the many miracles that guided me. I want to glorify God and encourage others to pursue their prophetic destiny directed by God.

This book uses my personal story, biblical principles and lifelong lessons to help others on their journey. It answers question about prophetic destiny as well as challenging false assumptions and unbiblical practices.

The emerging generation is wrestling for their journey for prophetic destiny. I write about Jacob who did not have clear direction from those who went before him. Jacob wrestled for his journey directed by God, but his parents, Isaac and Rebekah, didn't understand him. As a result, Jacob struggled without much help from his parents or anyone else. In my opinion, the current emerging generation is in the same situation and without much help. Many of us need to hear God's call to guide the next generation.

> Such is the generation of those who seek him, who seek your face, O God of Jacob.
>
> Psalm 24:6

I believe my personal testimony will help those who are struggling to discover their prophetic destiny. Many are striving by focusing on material provision such as wealth, success, fame, popularity, status, and power rather than cry out to the Lord like Jacob for true blessings that come with their true identity.

The objective is to show the journey for prophetic destiny is about entering into blessings and favor of God that He has prepared for us from the foundation of Earth by living in the center of His will. In this context, blessings include knowing who we are, whose we are and accepting responsibility to honor God by managing what He has given to each person. Hence, the journey for prophetic destiny is what merciful God preplanned for each individual to accomplish for His glory on Earth.

Therefore, true blessing is fulfilling what we are created, saved and anointed for. With this in mind, material provision is a means for the blessings we are created for. The foundation or the right starting point of the journey for prophetic destiny is relationship.

> This is my Son, whom I love; with him I am well pleased.
>
> Matthew 3:17

The goal is to glorify God. The Lord Jesus who started with God the Father finished His journey by declaring, "I have brought you glory on earth by completing the work you gave me to do" (John17:4). On the journey for prophetic destiny, the process of the journey is as important to God as much as the end result. Therefore, the key indicator of the journey's success on the journey is to do everything for the glory of God 24/7, as we become more like Christ.

In July 2017, I was invited to Melbourne, Australia to speak at a conference organized by Zion Church and Revival Church. Zion Church is an Amharic-speaking, Ethiopian church while Revival Church is English speaking. The Revival Church was established by Zion Church to reach Ethiopian-Australians whose language is English and culture is Australian. The unique things about this gathering were that attendees were young adults and Australians with an Ethiopian culture. The Church is for the emerging young generation, and the leaders are young people. The title of their conference was Breakthrough. I personally like the concept of breakthrough, because of its coloration with reaching the destination. I shared with the young people that if they haven't experienced breakout, it would be impossible to have breakthrough in their lives.

I changed their topic to "Breakout for Breakthrough." In other words, freedom for living life that we are created for. I started addressing this reality with the meaning of breakout which includes to advance, step forward, leap forward, step in the right direction, success, discovery, and finding some of the limiting factors in order to be free to envision the future.

Breakout is the first step toward true freedom to establish true identity in fulfilling the journey and reach the destination. Breakthrough includes an escape, an appearance, an instance of surpassing any previous achievement, a sudden increase, and as well as advancing to achieve the allotted goal. That is why I am writing about my journey for prophetic destiny.

In order to illustrate the nature, challenges, victories and fruits of fulfilling the journey, I shared my personal journey and life experiences as example with biblical truth. In the course of four days, I made an attempt to show the importance of living for their journey for prophetic destiny, and the need to understand the differences. Some differences are: popularity versus impact; prosperity versus blessings; breakout versus breakthrough. Reaching our destination is all about true spiritual freedom to live for the plan and purpose of God which are the greatest blessings and true prosperity, now and forever. That is called breakout for lasting breakthrough.

I like the example of an eagle. Eaglets must have breakout first from an egg. For an eagle, the egg is a very limiting place. It is a place of existence without any action or movement for a short time. It is a waiting place in the hope of having true freedom. Eaglets realize true freedom once they break out. For eaglets breaking out is a part of establishing true identity to advance. Eagles are created to fly and soar. They are created with that potential. But as long as an eaglet is in an egg, nothing happens. The problem is not for lack of potential, but lack of freedom. That is why without true breakout, breakthrough is just a distant dream. Reaching our destination is experiencing breakthrough to be, to will and to do because of the freedom. For an eagle, the greatest achievement is its ability to fly high since that is what it is created for. It starts with freedom from the confinement or limitation by breaking out. Young adults must know the importance of breakout to become true overcomers for lasting breakthrough in daily life.

After the conference, the young people asked me to take those points and write as it relates to my own personal journey to help this generation. They wanted to be shown the right starting place to reach the right destination. I accepted their challenge and promised to write my personal journey to illustrate and highlight some of the important aspects of our journey for lasting impact.

As I write *Breakout for Breakthrough: Journey for Prophetic Destiny,* my life story and ministry journey are a testimony to show the nature and purpose of a God-honoring, impactful journey toward the fulfillment of God's will on Earth. Everybody has a life journey. The only difference is the starting point, understanding the process and identifying the purpose, knowing or envisioning the final outcomes, and going on a life-long journey with a destination to honor God, impact generations and living life with God's purpose.

With spiritual determination and dedication to God, individuals are able to move from an ordinary Christian walk and ministry into an extraordinary relationship with the Lord to experience true blessings and make a greater impact in their spheres of influence.

Let me warn you!!! My journey may sound exciting, but it is filled with challenges. If you want to pursue the journey for your prophetic destiny, you will face many challenges. Some of those challenges will be difficult and not easy. Set your face into the strong wind of the enemy and push through with prayer and the power of the Holy Spirit. Your reward will be great, both on Earth and in Heaven.

BREAKOUT FOR BREAKTHROUGH

.

CHAPTER 1

NAMED FOR PROPHETIC DESTINY

A good name is more desirable than great riches; to
be esteemed is better than silver or gold.

Proverbs 22:1

The greatest prosperity, blessings and success come when we live for our prophetic destiny. Our prophetic destiny is what we are created for; God sets us apart for His purposes. In God's view, names are not just labels, but a description of purpose and true prophetic identity and life calling. When God names people, He affirms His eternal plan and purpose. Prophet Isaiah tells us that the Lord named him before he was born. That naming by God gave him authority as a prophet to declare the will and purpose of God to islands and nations. Prophet Jeremiah was set apart before he was born to be a prophet to the nations with authority; *over nations and kingdoms to uproot and tear down, to destroy and overthrow, to build and to plant.* In the context of covenant, when the Lord started blessing and prospering Abram and Sarai exceedingly,

He made them fruitful to establish His covenant with them, and He changed their names. "No longer will you be called Abram; your name will be Abraham, for I have made you a father of many nations…. As for Sarai your wife, you are no longer to call her Sarai; her name will be Sarah. I will bless her and will surely give you a son by her" (Genesis17;5,15-16). When Jacob cried for blessing and wrestled with the angel of the Lord as the sign of everlasting blessings and true prosperity, the Lord named him Israel.

The proper way to prosper is knowing and accepting our prophetic name and start living for that calling. When Jacob wrestled with the angel, he had a breakout for breakthrough. His name was changed to Israel, and he had a breakout from the old into the new. True prosperity can't be measured by our resources or wealth, but only by our true prophetic destiny directed by God. Resources are a means or instruments to live a prosperous life of glorifying and honoring God by doing everything for His glory. When we talk about prophetic names, we are not limited to names that have special meaning in specific languages, but in God's plan and purpose. In this context, the most important point is to know what we are created for, and we fulfill our calling by living the fullness of life that the Lord Jesus Christ came to give us. "I have come that they may have life, and have it to the full" (John 10:10). That is the true path to a lasting prosperity. A breakthrough into a powerful relationship with God.

His Name Is Beeftu

My grandparents lived in the remote part of central Ethiopia. They didn't have children for many years. When my grandmother had my father at an old age, she named him "Beeftu" saying, "I have seen the light at my old age." Beeftu means sun or dawn light. My father didn't have siblings; he grew up alone. Because of his loneliness and lifetime of struggle in poverty and his aged parents, he married my mother when they were very young. Even though they never told me how old they were when they were married, my guess is they were teenagers. They worked hard on a farm to survive and provide for nine children. They had ten children, but the ninth child died at birth. They overcame lack of basic necessities and were able to purchase farmland for my brothers.

Though there was no birth date recorded, my father lived a long life. According to my oldest brother's estimate, he died at 94 years. My father bought farming land for my older brothers, but he stayed in the same place and in an old grass hut. The only difference was that when I was young, I remember my father built a smaller grass hut, as a guest house. My father was not educated, poor as far as material wealth is concerned and never lived outside of his village. But very rich in wisdom and human relationship. Our home was like a courthouse. It was normal for neighbors to come with their issues, conflicts and disagreements. My father acted as a judge for our community. For some, he was only a judge, while for others he was a lawyer or advocate. He enjoyed farming and the reconciliation work for his community. He was very gentle, full of wisdom and highly respected in his community.

As a child, since I was the last one, I was very close to my father. I still remember some of the things that impacted me very much, because I watched my father. First, he was full of wisdom. Regularly people would come to him for advice. Second, he was a very gentle and peaceful man. I don't remember hearing my dad raising his voice in anger. Third, he was a very hard-working man, and he worked hard until the final days of his life. Fourth, he loved my mother and treated her with great respect and honor. He made sure all of us children respected and obeyed her. Fifth, he treated me with great respect. I don't know what he saw in me, but he would ask me for advice when I was very young. I remember, most evenings after everything became quiet, we would sit outside, and I talked with my dad for hours. He asked me things that he already knew. Now, looking back, he was educating me. That was the way he treated me and built self-confidence and determination in me. That was the greatest gift my father gave me as a young boy. My relationship with my father reminded me about the story of Joseph. The Bible describes the relationship between Jacob and Joseph. "Israel loved Joseph more than any of his other sons, because he had been born to him in his old age; and he made a richly ornamented robe for him" (Genesis 37:3). Joseph was amazing in that after his father gave him the garment of many colors that set him apart from his brothers, he started dreaming big dreams. The love, respect and covering of a father encourages young people to dream about their future because of self-confidence that is built in them. I felt that my father placed upon me a garment of prophetic destiny that separated me from my brothers and sisters just like Joseph.

After I earned my Ph.D. and many years passed, I was the keynote speaker at a major Christian conference in Chicago. At the end of my speech a Christian brother, who the Lord used mightily with signs and wonders in Ethiopia, raised his hand and said that he had a message for me from the Lord. He came to the stage and gave the following prophetic words, "I have set you apart from your brothers and put on you a garment of many colors just like Joseph." What my father, who didn't know the Lord, did when I was very young was confirmed by a national prophet on stage at a major conference. That was after the unforgettable experiences with my father, more than 20 years later.

Remember, my father's name is Beeftu, "morning light." The implication of morning dawn is not only for one person, but for everybody who would like to be the light. Somehow, my father wanted to see the reality of that in me, or through me, just like Jacob. But my heavenly Father made it a reality, by calling me to declare the light of his glorious Gospel to the nations. Others, like my father, may not have the biblical revelation for our lives; however, the Lord empowers them to make an impact on our lives for His purposes.

His Name Is Alemu

Like my father, I was born to my parents at their old age. As I have mentioned previously, I was born on an isolated farm in the Ethiopian countryside. I'm not quite sure when, because there is not a formal record of my birth. I was the youngest of ten children. After my older sister who was the ninth child died at birth, my mother didn't think she would have another child because of her age. After a number of years when she found out that she was expecting another child, it wasn't only a huge surprise, but also, she didn't like it. She told me that she felt ashamed to have a child at her age. She didn't want the pregnancy, because it was an embarrassment. She decided to abort it by taking local medicine. She consulted with her friends, and followed their instructions. But all the medicine she took into her body didn't affect me. Obviously, it didn't kill me as intended for the following reasons.

- The Lord saw me before my mother felt me. "Your eyes saw my unformed body."

- The Lord already planned out my days in advance before my mother found out that I was on the way. "All the days ordained for me were written in your book before one of them came to be."

- The Lord had named me before my mother found out that she was expecting me. "Before I was born the LORD called me; from my birth he has made mention of my name" (Isaiah 49:1). God named me for life and purpose; therefore, the medicine had no effect on me.

- The Lord had chosen me before I was conceived in my mother's womb and loved me before the foundation of the world. "For he chose us in him before the creation of the world to be holy and blameless in his sight in love"

(Ephesians 1:4). Therefore, the enemy was not able to kill me before I was born.

- The Lord called me and set me apart for His purpose before I was born, and nothing changes it. "The LORD Almighty has sworn, 'Surely, as I have planned, so it will be, and as I have purposed, so it will stand'" (Isaiah 14:24).

That is the story of my life in short!

The fact that I was born number ten is significant for me. In Genesis 1 is the phrase "God said" 10 times, which is a testimony of His creative power. God gave the 10 Commandments to mankind. Ten represents mankind's responsibility to keep the commandments. I have needed creative power in my life to overcome obstacles and fulfill His purpose.

The Lord shielded me from the enemy's hidden plan, and the time of birthing arrived. My mother gave birth to all her children at home. Since it was a countryside, no hospitals or clinics were available. The day I was born, my mother had an extremely difficult time. Probably it was difficult due to her old age. Possibly the difficulty was a foreshadow of the challenges I would face in my life. No matter the obstacles and hindrances, the enemy cannot stop us.

After that tough time when she was told that she had given birth to a boy and he is alive, she said, "His name is Alemu." Alemu means His world, meaning his everything or joy of life includes everything. In Amharic language, the Gospel of John 3:16 reads, "God so loved Alemu... ." meaning the people of the world that have been created for His glory. My mother named me Alemu to express her last joy of giving a birth to a boy after she lost a baby girl at birth. She said, "He is my last joy, and my world because the Lord gave me a son at my old age."

So, my legal name became Alemu Beeftu. In Ethiopian culture, we take our father's name as our last name. In other words, Alemu Beeftu means Alemu son of Beeftu. When I put together my name with my father's name, it uncovers the hidden prophetic destiny God purposed for my life before I was born. That is Alemu (His world) Beeftu (light). Jesus said, "You are the light of the world." The Lord Jesus called me and set me apart before the foundation of the world to be the messenger of the Gospel of Jesus Christ.

> That you may show yourselves to be blameless and guileless, innocent and uncontaminated, children of God without blemish (faultless, unrebukable) in the midst of a crooked and wicked generation [spiritually perverted and perverse], among whom you are seen as bright lights (stars or beacons shining out clearly) in the [dark] world.
>
> Philippians.2:15 AMP, emphasis added

That was the call on my life from the beginning, prophetically speaking.

As I have mentioned earlier, true and lasting or eternal prosperity, is fulfilling our prophetic destiny directed by God that reflects our true calling. That is living for the glory of God, loving our

God with everything that is in us and serving His purpose on Earth everyday of our lives. This is the proper path to prosperity. Prosperity doesn't start with provision, but with the true vision of who God is and who we are because of Him. A prosperous person is a person who has what he needs to live for the glory of God all the days of his life by redeeming the time.

My prophetic name is declaring the Gospel of His glorious light among the nations. Apostle Chuck Pierce described my calling to the nations this way.

You are called to have an apostolic sphere for the nations. You are called to unlock the harvest for the nations and for this nation. God is giving you strategy. You carry an experience of the glory of God and the principles of the glory of God that you can offer to people. Your sphere is the sphere of the glory of God in the nations. People need the glory of God and will ask you to help. They will submit to His glorious light and request you to be sent to accomplish this. You are able to help people to understand the power of His glory in almost any sphere because you carry it so strong within you. You are called to bring leaders into becoming glory carriers and those that receive it will unlock the harvest. Anybody that is aligning with you is looking for you to help them to become that.

I have believed and embraced this calling fully in my life. As a result, to this day the Lord has opened doors for me to declare His glory in more than 54 nations and many cities on six continents. My greatest fulfillment in life is living for my prophetic destiny by obeying His will wholeheartedly. Because of this, I feel that I am the richest, wealthiest person in the world. That is why I believe living for our prophetic destiny is the proper way to prosper. Breaking out for breakthrough into our prophetic destiny is available for each person who has a relationship with God, along with it we achieve our greatest fulfillment in life.

CHAPTER 2

WRESTLED FOR PROPHETIC

"I know the plans I have for you… plans to prosper
you and not to harm you, plans to give you hope and
a future."

Jeremiah 29:11

Since I was the last and youngest of ten children, I was expected to
stay on the family farm to help my father—and nothing more. My
parent's joy was to have a son at old age who would help them on the
family farm. Their expectation was for me to learn basic farming skills
and assist my father at that time and take over the responsibility one
day. I also accepted that assignment since it was all I knew when I was
growing into adulthood. However, the prophetic destiny God
preplanned for my life started making me restless without my
knowledge, like Jacob. Every person is born with God's preplanned
purpose, or *destiny* within them. Each person's purpose is prophetic as
God has called it into existence in advance; a uniquely planned or well-

orchestrated by the Creator Himself. In other words, God has a plan for you and me; just as He told the nation of Israel, "I know the plans I have for you… plans to prosper you and not to harm you, plans to give you hope and a future" (Jeremiah 29:11). Before Jacob was born, God declared over Jacob's destiny by saying,

> "The LORD said to her: "Two nations are in your womb; two people will come from you and be separated. One people will be stronger than the other, and the older will serve the younger."
>
> Genesis 25:23 HCSB

Jacob's first destiny was that Jacob would be a nation. The second, he would be stronger than other nations. Thirdly, his older brother would serve him. Jacob would be the leader. Although Jacob didn't understand the meaning, prophetic words started burning in his bones. As a result, he started fighting with his brother from birth. Jacob didn't stop wrestling until he encountered God both in Bethel and Peniel. Since it is the word spoken by God over our lives, our prophetic destiny is like a fire in our bones.

> If I say, "I will not mention him or speak any more in his name, his word is in my heart like a fire, a fire shut up in my bones. I am weary of holding it in; indeed, I cannot."
>
> Jeremiah 20:9

In short, that was my story as well. I didn't know what God had preplanned for life as I grew up. I didn't even know who God was in my early years. But I was always a curious child. I helped my father on the farm and was well-liked by my brothers and sisters. Since I was the baby in our family, my brothers and sisters treated me like their child, not like their brother. The oldest brother's first born was older than me. My mother nursed both of us. We grew up like twins.

When I was assisting my father with farming, a government-issued official letter occasionally made its way to our family farm. My father would carry that white piece of paper from the government and go around looking for someone who could read it to him.

One day I asked my father, "What is this thing you carry? Why does it make you look for someone?" My father answered, "I need someone who can tell me what is written on it." I responded, "What do I need to do to help you?"

My father replied, "You would have to go to a special place and learn how to read. One special place is where the Coptic Church priest lived. If you go there and spend time with a priest, he will show you or teach how to read what is on this white piece of paper. But you cannot do that. I need you on the farm. Your older brothers tried to do it, and they didn't like it. You wouldn't either. Besides, we cannot afford to send you to such a place." That was the day I saw a glimpse of my prophetic destiny or the future promise and hope. What my father said about the possibility of being able to read and understand what was on a white piece of paper ignited fire for knowing and how it related to learning in my life. I asked my father if I could do that for him, even though my brothers didn't like it. Finally, he let me go for a few weeks. But it was not formal school. When I look back now, I realize there was no schedule. No curriculum. Whenever the priest showed up, he asked me to repeat the Amharic alphabet after him, which didn't make any sense to me. I was discouraged and gave up the hope of helping my father by reading the tax paper that came from the government.

The First Miracle Toward My Destiny

The Lord started preforming miracles for me before I accepted the Lord Jesus Christ as my personal Savior. The first miracle was my mother's sister came to visit us at the right time. As I have mentioned, visiting a priest created in me a burning desire to learn how to read. Understand, I was about 12-years old at the time. Even though I didn't know anything about school or school age or what formal school was all about, that didn't affect my desire for learning how to read and write. That was a miracle by itself!

Because of my aunt's visit, I discovered a missionary school, about five to six hours' walk from my home, a place where I could learn to read. My aunt started telling me how children go school and learn in the Serving in Missions (SIM) that school was four miles from her home. I was so excited about the school. Even so I didn't have any clue about school, or what school looked like. I started talking with my aunt about a possibility of going with her, when she was returning home, so I could see the school for myself. She told me that I should ask my father if that would be acceptable to him. I told her he had already decided that I should help him on a farm. She told me that I couldn't go with her without his permission.

The circumstances were stacked against me. I was a mere farm boy. I had no money. My parents were against my learning anything apart from farming, and that meant farming as it had been done for generations. But I had a desire to read, and I was determined to do something about it that day. I returned to my aunt for further negotiation. At this time, I had already decided I could run away from home to go with her. I gave her the strategy of waiting for her somewhere in a field, of course, hiding from my parents, and go with her to see the school for myself and come back home on the following day. Because of my strong appeal, she agreed!. The day she left to return home, I left my family home very early and waited for her in the field and joined her on her journey home. For her, it was only returning home after she visited her sister and her family. But it was my first step into the unknown. The beginning of breakout for breakthrough was the first day I did something without my parent's knowledge or approval. I respected my parents but was compelled to take the first step. Moreover, I never walked that long in my life. It was the longest journey from home as well as from what I was familiar with. Literally, on that day I took a journey of a lifetime by walking away from everything I knew, and what I was expected to do and be. Without knowing its full implication, it was the day I took a step of faith toward my prophetic destiny by letting go of my past for the sake of the future and the known for the sake of unknown. That is the entry point not only for me, but for everyone who would like to move into their promised hope or future that we call our prophetic destiny.

God honors and works with our determination not with our wishes. That was what Ruth, in the Book of Ruth in the Bible, did when she refused to bow down to idols. She stood strong in worshipping God and started her journey with Naomi to the unknown future with the strength of her mind and determination. She became part of the lineage of the Lord Jesus, even though she was a Moabite. A key component for the journey of our prophetic destiny is determination to enter into the future by faith.

The Second Miracle

I was admitted to school without proper timing or qualification. A missionary overruled the school system to accept me in the middle of the school year without my having a knowledge of the language. After more than a half-day journey with my aunt, we had arrived at her place. I spent the night. That was the first night I spent outside of my home. The next day, she told me to go across a river, that was very near to her home, and look for a big compound that was fenced with wire. She also said, "The houses have tin roofs and that will be a sign for you. When you see these, that is the school where children go to learn how to read and write. You will tell me what you think before you go back to your parents." I agreed and left her home. I had never seen a house with a tin roof before, so I didn't know what to expect. I found the compound and entered through a big gate. But I didn't see children. What I didn't realize was that children were in classrooms when I arrived. I didn't know anything about classrooms, starting time or end time or about a school year, for that matter. I went there in the middle of the school year after students had started classes.

Though I didn't see anybody, I kept looking around. Finally, I saw a very small office. The door was halfway open. I decided to go in the door and see. When I came closer and looked inside, I saw something I had never seen before. A lady with a white face! Like many other firsts, it was the first time I saw a white person. I assumed everybody was like me. My learning curve started right away by realizing some people have different skin colors than mine, black. I had not heard that people were born with different skin colors. At least I had known about another language other than my mother tongue, which is Oromigna, a Cushitic language of the Afro-Asiatic family.

The white face I saw in the office was the missionary who was the director of the school. She tried to speak in Amharic, the national language, to find out what I was looking for. But I didn't know that another language was spoken other than my mother tongue, let alone speaking it. I tried my best not only using my language, but also with my body language to tell her that I was there to learn how to read and write. I was desperate and eager for her to know how much I want to learn. After she saw my desperation instead of giving me a sign to go away, she gave a sign to wait. She went to one classroom and brought a teacher with her. He was an Oromigna speaker and asked what I wanted. I told him that I came all the way from my village to learn how to read and write.

After the lady heard my story, she waited a few minutes without saying anything and looked at me. It felt like an eternity because of my anguish. By taking time to look at me, she was looking at the passion that I brought with me in spite of all the challenges I was facing; poverty, distance, lack of knowledge and language. I only knew the language of my native region. To go to school, I would need to learn Amharic, the national language of Ethiopia. I had already lost half a year since it was in the middle of the year. She was also looking into my determination and potential for learning. Whether she knew it or not, she realized my prophetic destiny at that instant and made a major risky decision.

First, for admittance into the school in the middle of the year without language knowledge. After she looked at me for few minutes, she instructed the teacher who was interpreting, "Take him to first grade." When she said to follow him to the classroom, he was as surprised as I was!

Second, to overrule the school admission rule. The mission rule for the school was to admit new students in September, the beginning of the school year. I never knew how she justified the decision or what kind of repercussions she received for admitting me. But I am here today because of her decision many years ago. Maybe she was merely fulfilling her God-given assignment as a missionary to Ethiopia. I don't know if she authored any books during her lifetime. By admitting me into the school, she is like a co-author with me for more than 40 books. I don't know if she ever led anyone to the Lord. But through the ministry, Gospel of Glory, more than 3,000 receive the Lord every year. I don't know if she has travelled to countries in addition to the U.S. and Ethiopia. But she has been with me as I have travelled to more than 54 nations by admitting me into the school. That is 54 nations and with plans to minister in more nations.

The Third Miracle

The Lord opened my mind and gave me understanding. The teacher placed me in the first class and went back to teach his class. I didn't have proper clothes on, and every child was looking at me. Since I didn't know the language, I didn't understand anything that was going on including the instructions. But I was fascinated with everything, and I didn't want to give up and return to the farm. I went back to my aunt's home, and she asked how it went. With great excitement, I told her about the school and my classroom experience, although I didn't understand anything. I just wanted to return. In the meantime, my father discovered what had happened. But the Lord softened my father's heart, and he sent a message saying that I could continue in school for a while. He started sending supplies to my aunt to support me in school.

The greatest miracle started taking place in my life. The Lord opened my mind, and I started understanding the language and subjects. Before long, I became part of the class. At the end of the school year, I was second in my class. Remember, I was in school only half the school year. It was a miracle! That process led me not only to start reading and writing, but also to higher education years later.

To break the poverty cycle, education and lack of knowledge were addressed in my life. The education placed me on the path of a proper way to prosper. I was realizing the potential the Lord had deposited in me; my prophetic destiny for the glory of His name. Breakout for breakthrough breaks us out of cycles that hold us back from achieving our prophetic destiny.

CHAPTER 3

JOURNEY FOR PROPHETIC DESTINY

What will it benefit a man if he gains the whole world yet loses his life? Or what will a man give in exchange for his life?

Matthew16:26

Starting My Journey with God

My parents attended a Coptic Church once in a while for religion ceremonies, but the Word of God was not taught. Because of lack of knowledge regarding what Christianity is all about, my parents and all my community mixed this religion's rituals with idol worship. They didn't know the difference between worshiping God and idols. However, my mother said all the time, "The fear of God." That word became part of me, even though I didn't know which God we were worshiping. Did I want to fear and revere the gods my parents worshiped at home or the One at the Coptic Church where we would pray once in a while? I didn't have an answer.

Sir, What Is the Answer?

God was clearing the way for me. He opened not only my eyes to see my reality, spiritual speaking, but He opened my heart to accept the Lord as my personal Savior in an unusual setting. Come to think about it, nothing is usual about my life's journey. When I was in second grade, a math teacher read Psalm 15 as an opening to class. Verse one was written to ask my life question before I was born, "LORD, who may dwell in your sanctuary? Who may live on your holy hill?" (Psalm 15:1). I knew I couldn't dwell in the presence of God. The Lord opened my eyes, and for the first time showed me what hell is all about. I was sitting by a small window. I began to shake. I was shaking all through class. I tried my best to control my body from shaking, but I wasn't able. I knew I had to do something in response to the God of this Psalm. After class, I asked the math teacher about what he'd read. I said, "Sir, what is the answer to what you read?" He told me not to worry about it because it wasn't part of the curriculum. He said, "I just felt to read it." I figured out that he didn't understand not only my question, but also my desperation to find the answer.

I searched for the missionary who had helped me. At that time, the director of the school had left for Australia to take a one-year break from the mission field. However, Bea Colman was in charge of the school. I asked her about Psalm 15. I didn't even tell her my class experience. She understood what was happening, and she shared the Gospel with me sitting under the flagpole surrounded by students.

After she explained the Gospel and the way of salvation, she asked me if I would like to accept the Lord as my personal Savior. I replied, "Yes, I would." She said, "Let us go to one of the classrooms, and I will pray with you." To her surprise, I said, "No." She asked, "Didn't you say, 'I would like to accept the Lord as my Savior?'" "Yes, I still would like to do that. But if everything you said is true, I don't want to wait until I make sure I am saved." She read Romans10:9, "If you confess with your mouth, 'Jesus is Lord, and believe in your heart that God raised him from the dead, you will be saved.'" After that she led me in prayer, and I accepted the Lord for the first time. I was about 14 at the time. That day I gave my life to Christ, and it marked a turning point in my life toward my prophetic destiny. My journey for my prophetic destiny with God and for God started that day. Even so I didn't understand the full implication of my decision that placed me on a true path to prosperity by breaking the cursed generation for the first time. I was experiencing breakout from the past. I am the first person in my family who went to formal school as well as accepting the Lord Jesus Christ as my Lord and Savior. That was the true starting day of my prophetic destiny. Until we have a true relationship with God through the forgiveness of sin, we haven't started much of anything.

What I have just mentioned in the above paragraph is called becoming a new creation by being born again. This is the foundation of every true prosperity and heavenly blessings. We are created and redeemed to be blessed and becoming a blessing through our relationship with God. That is how we step into our role in the Kingdom of God; that is managing Earth and all that God created in five days for His glory.

Journey of Restoration of Prosperity

Our redemption is the activation of our journey for the prosperity that God created for us and called us for at the beginning. Genesis is the beginning of, if not all things, most things that we understand in creation. The order of creation shows the original design or blueprint God established for His glory in order to prosper His people. The greatest blessings in creation were to be created in the image and after the likeness of God. "Then God said, 'Let us make man in our image'" (Genesis 1:28). He created us to be like Him in everything for the glory and honor of His holy name. No greater blessings, prosperity or success exists than being created in the image of God and receiving His breath, forgiveness of sins and eternal life. This salvation and relationship have been secured forever by the sealing and indwelling of Holy Spirt. This released all spiritual blessings not only in the heavenly realm in Christ Jesus, but also on Earth by removing the enemy of prosperity, the curse of sin. Yes, since our God is the source of all blessings and prosperity, He created us to be like Him, and He bestowed upon us all these things for His glory.

The proper path to all prosperities is a right relationship with Him, which moves us from an ordinary, material-focused lifestyle into an extraordinary relationship with our heavenly Father, who is the creator and sustainer of everything by the power of His word. This is more than only having abundantly what we want or desire, it is walking in the authority of God who gave us in creation. "You made them rulers over the works of your hands; you put everything under their feet" (Psalm 8:6). In this context, prosperity is more than accumulating things, it is managing things in divine order for the glory of the Creator as we fulfill His will on Earth. It is ruling things, rather than being ruled and controlled by our wants. In this case, prosperity is having what we need more than what we want. What we need is divine power to rule Earth for the glory of God.

In addition, the pattern of creation also shows us how much God wants mankind to prosper in the proper way and manner. After He created the heavens and Earth, in the beginning before He created mankind, He restored the formless and empty Earth into a beautiful planet and gave it to mankind, a living creature in His image, in the Garden of Eden.

All five-day creation is for human beings. He didn't only create everything for mankind, but also made mankind to take charge of all His creation. He gave them dominion to rule and manage the entire Earth. He blessed them, Adam and Eve, to multiply and be fruitful. As such, the first communication God had with them, after they became one, was blessings. That is to prosper in everything. Furthermore, He commanded them to fill all Earth with these blessings and prosperity. Can you imagine living on Earth? The continent, country, region, and community filled with all the blessings of God and prospering continually. When God placed them in the Garden of Eden, it is written, "The LORD God took the man and put him in the garden of Eden to tend and keep it" (Genesis 2:15). That was God's plan and desire for human beings.

Poverty and lack were never part of God's plan for us. That is the plan and desire of the enemy, who came to kill and destroy what is good, fruitful and prosperous. Satan, our enemy, uses many ways and methods to destroy the blessings and prosperity God intended for us to have at creation.

Poverty Came In

The foundation of prosperity and all blessings is our relationship with the Creator, owner and sustainer of everything. Broken relationship is an enter point for poverty. The question has been if, in fact, we were created for blessings and to prosper. "How then did we end up at where we are?" Of course, it is opposite to the original plan of God. The simple answer is the enemy, satan, deceived Adam and Eve into disobeying God. When they rebelled against God's plan and purpose for their lives, their relationship was broken. That opened the door for the curse rather than blessings. However, at creation they received the blessings of prosperity and multiplication from God because of their relationship with God, the Creator. He declared blessings upon them. "God blessed them and said to them, 'Be fruitful and increase in number'" (Genesis 1:28).

Prosperity and increase were the result of God's pronouncement upon them. Note, God didn't pronounce the blessings on Earth, but upon mankind who was created to carry His image and rule on Earth. However, after Adam and Eve sinned and their relationship was broken, the Lord cursed Earth, not the mankind first, but the source of their prosperity by saying, "Cursed is the ground because of you" (Genesis 3:17). Poverty replaced prosperity because of mankind's disobedience. Mankind was given authority to rule Earth by obeying God.

Yes, poverty is the result God's curse. The two aspects of curses are trying to be like God and desiring what belongs to God. Taking what God told them not to eat was greed for more without lack or hunger. Such lack of honoring God and lack of contentment leads into the love of money, or resources more than God, which is the root of all evil. The Word of God, in the New Testament, describes it this way,

> People who want to get rich fall into temptation and a trap and into many foolish and harmful desires that plunge men into ruin and destruction. For the love of money is a root of all kinds of evil.
>
> 1 Timothy 6:9-10

We are created to love God with everything that is within us and worship Him and honor Him with our firstfruits. In other words, we overcome the love of money by honoring God in our tithing and firstfruits (Proverbs 3:9). In addition, He told His people to come before Him, three times a year for celebrations; the Feasts of Passover, Harvest and the Ingathering. The Ingathering is the term used by the Jews for the return of Jews to Israel.

Signs of Poverty

In Genesis, the poverty manifested in life is in a number of ways. For example:

- **Spiritual Poverty**

Spiritual poverty is separation from God which is spiritual death. The worst form of poverty, since the consequence of spiritual separation from God, is both physical death and eternal judgment. "Just as man is destined to die once, and after that to face judgment" (Hebrews 9:27). This is loss of life, freedom, peace and eternal suffering in hell without having any relationship with God. It is the result of spiritual poverty. That is why the Lord Jesus taught, if mankind loses his life and gains all the material of this world, it does not benefit him anything.

The beginning of the restoration of prosperity is reestablishing our relationship with God through repenting. Accepting the Lord Jesus Christ as personal Lord and Savior releases spiritual blessings by removing the curses of sin and iniquity of the past. The Lord Jesus came so we are able to receive abundant life. The measurement of true prosperity is not having what we want, but to receive from God what we need, which is eternal and abundant life. What makes this point so important is that we are created in His image for everlasting relationship and to enjoy the blessings of walking with God. Genesis 5:24 shows us how important this is to God, creation and covenant. "Enoch walked with God; then he was no more, because God took him away."

- **Relational Poverty**

When Adam sinned, his vertical relationship also affected his horizontal relationship with his wife. The greatest wealth is true and rich human relationship, particularly with family members. However, the foundation of our relationship with others is the reflection of relationship with God. For example, Adam and Eve, when they had right standing with God, Adam said about Eve, "The man said, 'This is now bone of my bones and flesh of my flesh; she shall be called 'woman,' for she was taken out of man'" (Genesis 2:23). After his personal relationship with God was broken with the same mouth, "The man said, 'The woman you put here with me—she gave me some fruit from the tree, and I ate it'" (Genesis 3:12). This is the same man who confessed their unity and equality. Sin of disobedience brought about relational poverty breakdown, which is the worst form of poverty.

Some years ago, I conducted a special leadership workshop in Brazil for 30 major business owners in a newly built mall. In this leadership group, all morning I shared with the participants some business and leadership principles to grow their business. In the afternoon, each person came up with a business plan for expansion. The excitement was great! They kept asking me where I found these amazing leadership principles for effectiveness in business. I kept promising them that I would share the information sources at the end.

Finally, I asked them to share their five-year expansion plan and what each company will be worth in five years. Each leader shared with great excitement their projections. I continue on and asked them to share on the same graph what the condition of their family would look like in five years as they focused on the expansion of their companies and growing the businesses. Suddenly, the room became very quiet. Some started struggling emotionally. At the conclusion, most said if they continued putting as much time and energy into the growth and expansion of their business for the next five years, most likely, they would end up in divorce and their children would be drug addicts. I asked a simple question, "Is that prosperity or success?" All of them replied, "No!" At that stage I shared the resources of my information, the Bible, and quoted for them one verse, "What will it benefit a man if he gains the whole world yet loses his life? Or what will a man give in exchange for his life?" (Matthew 16:26). At this point, all of them chose a true prosperity which is a personal relationship with God and family. As the result, all of them invited the Lord Jesus Christ into their lives. When we are in a right relationship with God and others, the blessings are already commanded,

> How good and pleasant it is when brothers live together in unity. For there the LORD bestows his blessing, even life forevermore.
>
> Psalm.133:1, 3

- **Physical Poverty**

Physical poverty is lack of provision because of disobedience. When Adam and Eve sinned, the Lord cursed Earth. The curse of Earth is manifested in producing the wrong things. The Lord said, "Cursed is the ground because of you; ... It will produce thorns and thistles for you" (Genesis 3:17-18). Since then throughout the Bible, the result of turning way from God opens doors to curses, as a form of God's judgment. Poverty is not a gift from our loving heavenly Father, but the fruit of rebelling against the will and purpose of God.

In my case, the day I accepted the Lord, the generational curse was broken. I became a new creation. What was taken from my family, because of separation from God, is now being restored through the Lord Jesus Christ who broke the curse of the generations by becoming sin for me.

> Christ redeemed us from the curse of the law by becoming a curse for us, for it is written: "Cursed is everyone who is hung on a tree. He redeemed us in order that the blessing given to Abraham might come to the Gentiles through Christ Jesus, so that by faith we might receive the promise of the Spirit."
>
> Galatians 3:13-140

In this sense, prosperity begins when we come back to our original place and purpose to rule Earth for His glory. Authority for ruling Earth is a responsibility of managing the creation. Prosperity is not a resource ownership but managing for the Owner and Creator. The blessing is the reward of honoring the Owner for all. That is the core of our prophetic destiny since we are created and redeemed for this.

CHAPTER 4

CHALLENGES FOR PROPHETIC DESTINY

Therefore, come out from among them and be separate, says the Lord; do not touch any unclean thing, and I will welcome you.

2 Corinthians 6:17

The journey for our prophetic destiny encounters many challenges. Since our prophetic destiny is what God created and saved for us, the kingdom of darkness opposes us with all its forces. Looking at Old Testament times, the journey of the Jewish people is an excellent example for such challenges. Pharaoh, king of Egypt, refused to let them go into their promised land. But the promised land was their prophetic destiny. The Lord had promised their father Abraham, 430 years ago. The Lord brought them out with a mighty army, preforming ten signs and wonders. Even after they came out, Pharaoh didn't want to give up, but followed them to the Red Sea.

My personal journey is not much different. I faced a number

of challenges that tried to stop me or forced me to go back. I had started to rebuild my relationship with my family after running away from home. My father accepted the reality and began supporting me by sending supplies to my aunt. Everything was going very well until my family found I accepted the Lord as my personal Lord and Savior.

Escaped My Father's Spear

The conflict that came between us happened during Christmas break. For the holidays I went home where the family's traditional celebrations were in process. All my brothers and sisters were home. A sheep was slaughtered and prepared for us, and the family stood in line to receive a portion. This was a Christmas celebration that was mixed with idol worship. Recently, I had accepted Christ as my personal Savior and accepted salvation. I didn't have very much knowledge about idol worship. However, I felt in my heart very strongly not to eat the meat my father was giving to all my siblings as blessed food that had been offered to the idol they worshiped. Since I am the youngest, I was the last in line. I respected my father. He was normally a gentle, quiet man. But when my turn to receive a portion from the sheep came, I could not take it. I felt this following verse without really knowing its meaning.

> Come out from among them and be separate, says the Lord; do not touch any unclean thing, and I will welcome you.
>
> 2 Corinthians 6:17

When my father saw that I was not coming to take the meat, he started wondering. He said, "Come and take it." I responded with an unwise word and tone of voice by saying, "Now, I am a Christian, and I don't want to eat what is offered to an idol." My father believed that he was a Christian in spite of mixing traditional religion with idol worship. They worshiped idols because of fear.

He became livid with rage and reached for his spear. My own father who I had dearly loved in my growing up years was about to kill me! He picked up his spear. But, thankfully, one of my brothers intervened, saying, "He's only a boy! You can discipline him and get him to change his mind. You don't have to kill him!" I left the presence of my father. I was afraid to see him.

But during the rest of the vacation time, I had to avoid my father. He continued in his anger. He made a decision that I shouldn't go back to the missionary school. When I was told that he would not let me go back to school, I didn't know what to do. I was a newborn believer and was beginning to read the Bible, but I knew I had to pray. Since I didn't have a place of prayer, I would go and hide in a forest of banana trees and pray. That was my upper room for prayer for many years. During the rainy season because of the mud, it was very difficult to kneel for prayer. Truthfully, I didn't know if God could hear me if I prayed standing up. I would kneel in that muddy, wet place. But I had the greatest joy of my life because I knew prayer worked. After I prayed for the remainder of Christmas break, I was not ready to give up my education. But I was determined to return to school even without my father's approval and support. Somehow, I knew this would be about my future, my prophetic destiny, as written in this book. At the end of the vacation, I went back to the school without telling my parents.

When I returned to school, my aunt, who had been giving me room and board, soon found out about the incident. She waited a few days for the supply to be sent from my parents. In the meantime, my aunt's husband organized a special celebration and worship night for his idols. He asked me to help with the preparation for the special idol worship night. I told him that since I am a believer in the Lord Jesus Christ, I didn't want to help him in the worship of false gods. Because I was living in his house, it didn't go well with him. He told my aunt that I couldn't stay any longer. She told me that night, I couldn't come back to her home after school. She said, "You no longer can live under my roof." That was the most challenging night of my life. The next morning, I decided to go to school for the last time, even though I didn't know what would happen after school.

When I arrived at school in the morning, I tried to pretend everything was well. However, it wasn't long before the school director, who was also my teacher, noticed that something was bothering me. Finally, she got the story out of me. She told me about a nearby dorm available for boys who lived far from the school. She arranged for me to work for her every day after school and on weekends in order to pay for my food and other expenses.

Can I Have My Bible Now?

School, food and housing were covered the day I started working for her. But I had a very strong desire to be able to buy a Bible. I told her the day I started working about my plan to save money to buy a Bible. As a new believer, I was hungry for the Word of God more than anything. The school director told me I could earn that, too. However, a schoolboy who needs to work for his schooling doesn't end up with much extra money. One year later, I still did not have a Bible. I went to the director who counted my money and discovered I only had half of the required amount. When she told me, I was so sad and disappointed. I started envisioning another year without reading the Word of God. Because of the depth of my disappointment, tears started running down my cheeks. When she saw that, she asked me if it was because of a Bible. I told her, "Yes, that is the reason." She gave me a Bible that evening. What a joyful night! Another student and I were sharing a small room. That night I didn't sleep; I read my new Bible all night long. My roommate was very unhappy with me, but I didn't pay much attention. I loved the Word of God. I am still reading it. I am not a theologian, but I love the Word of God.

Walking 10 Miles for Sunday school

A teachable spirit is one of the key elements in breakout from the old and entering into the new. Yes, I started reading the Word of God the night I received my Bible, but as a new believer I had a strong desire to know and learn the Word of God. One morning Mrs. Colman started teaching in discipleship class. She called it Sunday school. We were five in number, but she prepared lessons as if she taught a very large, important class. My challenge was during summer when school was closed. During summer, I stayed in the countryside and helped my father on the farm. That means I didn't have the opportunity to attend my Sunday school class. But since I did not want to miss Sunday school, I would get up very early in the morning. It was dark, and I walked for about 10 miles without telling my parents about church. It was rainy season, and it rained on me. I went to the toilet room and twisted my clothes to remove some water. I put on the same clothes and attended both Sunday school and church before returning home. Upon arrival home, I went straight to the herds and came home with the cows after dark. This was without eating any food all day.

Why Do You Teach My Word?

The night I received my Bible and started reading it, I loved it so much I didn't want to stop reading. The first time when a teacher asked me to share for school devotions, I didn't have a Bible. I didn't know the difference between the Old and New Testaments. I didn't close the Bible I had borrowed until I finished sharing, since I didn't know how to find a passage of scripture in the Bible. That day I made a decision to know the scriptures. I also promised the Lord to keep my passion for the Word of God as long as I live.

I started ministry with a very high level of commitment and fire for the Word of God. After many years had passed, I was invited to speak at a conference in Rome, Italy. As I was flying to Rome, I started reading a book about the Word of God and true worship. I had just started writing a book in Amharic, *True Worship*. My reading was a part of the research I was doing for the book I started writing. While I was enjoying the reading, I heard an inner voice that was saying *stop reading.* I was puzzled and stopped reading for a few minutes and restarted again. I heard the same voice again. I started paying attention. After a few minutes, the same voice said, *Where are you going?* I thought I had a wonderful answer, so I responded, "I am going to Rome." The same voice came back with another question, "Why do you go to Rome?" I answered by saying, "To speak at a spiritual conference." There was silence for a few minutes again. At this time, I knew the Lord was speaking to me. I started weeping, forgetting that I was flying with other passengers in a plane. The presence of the Lord was so real! I didn't know how to respond or how to be. The same voice asked me, *Why do you preach my word? Do you preach it because you know how to preach, or do you preach because you love my word?* I lost it! I was reminded about the night I received my Bible, and the first time I preached by borrowing a Bible.

When I arrived in Rome, the pastor who invited me arrived to pick me up and asked if I would like to stop to eat. I replied, "No, but thank you. Just take me to the hotel." After he dropped me off, he asked me what time I would like to eat dinner. I told him that I wouldn't need dinner and to come back tomorrow. As soon as he left, I was on my face on the floor. I didn't change my clothes. As I was repenting and praying, I fell asleep. At 2 a.m., I was awakened and told by a voice to read Leviticus 6:8-13.

When I opened the passage and read it, three times the same warning and command was given to the Levites. "Do not let the fire go out on the altar of God." That night I understood the importance of keeping the fire burning. One of the greatest challenges during the journey of our prophetic destiny is keeping the fire burning. When the fire of love, Holy Spirit, holiness, worship, the Word of God, and ministry have burned out, the journey for our prophetic destiny is all about the title without lasting impact. Strong wish and desire without true breakthrough. A person can have a title but is not able to fulfill everything that goes along with the title.

After I received my Bible by working for the missionary, Miss Ruth Cane, we became very close. She was like a mother to me. I wanted to continue my education by working for her. However, I faced two challenges. The first challenge was that the mission elementary school was only through fourth grade. That means I had to go public school in the town of Waliso, about four miles from the mission school. I applied for fifth grade at Rase Gobena Dachew High School and was accepted. The second challenge is if the missionary lady would allow me to continue working for her and stay in the same dorm while attending public school. Finally, I asked Miss Ruth Cane. She told me that she would be going back to Australia for a year's vacation, but she would ask the replacement person as the director of the school. I expressed my gratitude for her help and support, and she left. I started working for the new lady that summer and started fifth grade at public school in the fall. The year went very good until the end of school. After I completed fifth grade, the missionary lady told me that she would not let me work for her as I go into sixth grade. In Ethiopian school system, sixth grade is very important. At the end of sixth grade, everyone who would like to continue in an academy is required to take the national exam and pass with a good grade. I really wanted to attend school so I could take the national exam.

I didn't know how to overcome that challenge. I did two things. I continued praying and refused to give up hope. During summer break, I happened to see the teacher who helped me the first time, when I went to school to learn how to read and write. I shared my situation. After he heard my concerns and desire to continue in school, he said he had an answer for me, if I was serious. I told him I am very serious about my education. He asked me if I would be willing to go to another part of the country to continue my education. I rsponded, "Yes!" He told me about an elementary teacher who had been transferred from that area to a place called Borre in Sidamo, Ethiopia. He said that he would like to have a Christian brother who could stay with him and go to the same school where he was teaching. I told him that I would go gladly. He told me that he would buy the bus tickets, and it would be two days' journey. We set a date, I showed up that day, and he gave me the bus tickets. I had never been to the area, and I didn't know anything about it, but I was determined. I made it after two days travelling. I attended sixth grade staying with him, took the national exam and passed with a very high score.

Do You Remember Me?

My relationship with Miss Cane was significant and greatly influenced my life's journey. She transferred from Waliso to another region in Ethiopia, and she invited me to go to that school, and also work for her. When I told a missionary, who was in charge, he said, "No." She needed his permission to for me to go where she was. I was very disappointed, but the Lord gave this verse, "No discipline seems pleasant at the time, but painful. Later on, however, it produces a harvest of righteousness and peace for those who have been trained by it" (Hebrews 12:11). After I received my Ph.D. when I was working for Compassion International, I went to Australia to conduct a leadership training workshop. After the workshop, I took a few days off to look for Miss Cane in Sydney, Australia. I looked for almost for a day and found her in a retirement place. My first question was to her was, "Do you remember me?" Her answer was, "Oh, yes!" I thanked her for everything and particularly for the Bible. I told her, "I earned my Ph.D. from Michigan State University, and I am working for an international organization that works with children." I took her out for dinner, and we had wonderful time. She didn't have words to thank the Lord and express her heartfelt gratitude that I had looked for her and shared what the Lord has done. She felt that the Lord sent me to tell her that her work was not in vain.

I Don't Want to See You Here Again!

The school I attended for sixth grade did not go beyond the sixth grade. I had to go back to Waliso, my hometown, for middle school. I went to the school where I attended fifth grade to register for seventh grade. To my surprise, I was told that they didn't have space for me. I went to the school director's office to appeal and plead with the school director. He told me the same thing. Since I was determined not to give up, I decided to go every morning and sit at his office door. The first day he asked me what I was doing at his office door. I told him that I would like to be admitted to school. He said, "I don't want to see you here again!" Again, I refused to give up. I decided to borrow books and notebooks from my friends to make copies every night and sit at the director's office door to study all day. Every time he saw me , he kept saying "I don't want to see here again!" I did the same thing every day from the middle of September until the end of October.

One day he was very upset with me and called me into his office to give me the last warning. Before he did, he asked if I had my results with me. Since, I was carrying my sixth-grade, national exam results, I handed it to him. When he saw the results, he was stunned. He said, "Why didn't you tell me about the high score?" I didn't respond. He told me to follow him. He picked up a chair from his office and carried it to seventh grade and told me to sit. He told the class teacher I would be an additional student in her class.

The classroom teacher was from Chicago who came as part of a national service. She was very offended by what the school director did. She thought I would be behind by almost a month and half. But she didn't know about my copying class notes and studying diligently. She gave us an exam the same day morning. My score was the second highest in the class. She thought I had copied it from some other students. After class was dismissed, she told me to stay behind for another exam. I took the test and scored even higher. After that her attitude toward me changed, and she liked me very much.

Determination and refusing to give up hope are the core issues on a journey of our prophetic destiny. Challenges are not to stop us but to strengthen and build our character for the future responsibility.

CHAPTER 5

CHALLENGES OF FAITH FOR PROPHETIC DESTINY

Jacob called the place Peniel, saying, "It is because I saw God face to face, and yet my life was spared."

Genesis 32:30

My seventh-grade experience was wonderful. I met bright students, and we became very close friends. But life outside of school became extremely difficult. I didn't have a support system in school. I went home on Friday and came back on Sunday. My mother would bake me a local bread that I lived on for a week. After a few days, the bread becomes dry and hard to eat. Since I didn't have anything else, I poured salt into water, dipped a piece of bread and ate it. Other times, I went early in the morning and collected dry coffee tree leaves to boil, and I poured salt into it so I could eat. It became even harder when I didn't have money to pay my share of the rent.

If You Want to Go to School…?

Finally, I decided to start looking for some support. I approached my history teacher, from the nation of India. He had a servant court, and I could stay with them. I was excited and told him I would do anything after school and on the weekend to help around the house, except for Sunday morning. On Sunday morning, I would like to go to church. He told me that was not a problem, and they didn't need much help.

I moved into their servant court and started helping his wife. They had a big water tank, and his wife would tell me if I wanted to go school, I had to fill it up by piping it. She didn't want to use electric power to fill it up. I did that every morning. In the evening after school, I washed and waxed the floor. She would say, "I can't see my face. The floor is not shiny enough. You have to do it until I can see the reflection of my face." At night, she asked me to take thread that she had purchased and make it into balls to make sweaters. It was very time-consuming work. In order to go to school, I had to finish by the morning. I did everything she asked so I could continue in school. However, her husband didn't know any of these things.

The Lord used this experience to teach me determination, resolve, persistence and focus. Without these characteristics and traits, it's impossible to reach our prophetic destiny. This is also the way for breakthrough and the proper way to prosperity. Hardworking and diligent in what we are given is what brings honor and glory to the Lord. Laziness is the enemy of our prophetic destiny. Jacob fought for his prophetic destiny by servicing with his labor for Laban for 20 years. "God has seen my hardship and the toil of my hands, and last night he rebuked you" (Genesis 31:42). The Lord blessed Jacob, made him prosperous and brought him back to Bethel, the place of his prophetic destiny. The Lord used that long process to bring Jacob to Peniel. "Jacob called the place Peniel, saying, 'It is because I saw God face to face, and yet my life was spared'" (Genesis 32:30).

The effective journey of our prophetic destiny is to reach a place where we see God and hear His voice. The face of God! There is no greater blessing and genuine prosperity than seeing the face of God. "Seek the Lord and His strength; yearn for and seek His face and to be in His presence continually!" (Psalm 105:4). Seeking the face of God is all about a transforming relationship with Him. If we don't actively seek Him, we won't find Him. Breaking out into breakthrough is a result of pressing into God and being in His presence.

Jacob had been on a journey to find his prophetic destiny since birth. Finally, at Peniel he received a new name as a sign of blessing from God, and a breakthrough to reach his destination. He pressed onward for many years before he reached Peniel, where he saw God, face to face.

Peniel means "the face of God." The face of God is about His presence; His majesty, His glory, and His power. Seeking the face of God is the ultimate goal for a generation with a prophetic destiny like Jacob's. He arrived at his prophetic destiny after a special encounter with God.

Moses spent 40 days and nights on a mountain in the presence of God. When he came down from the mountain, his face was shining with God's glory.

ɪ we seek God's hand, we seek provision and relate to
rovider, Guide, Deliverer, Protector, et al. His role in our
ɪives is that He is the Good Shepherd. We enter into such a covenant
relationship by knowing Him and accepting Him as our Savior and
High Priest. That is the foundation of our salvation.

When we seek His face, we relate to him as our King and Lord
to honor and worship Him. We declare not only what He does for us,
but who He is and what He deserves as our Creator, Redeemer, Lord
and King.

> To him who sits on the throne and to the Lamb be
> praise and honor and glory and power, for ever and
> ever! The four living creatures said, "Amen," and the
> elders fell down and worshiped.
>
> Revelation 5:13-14

Seeking God is about the true desire to exalt Him through worship. A
true desire creates a burning passion to be in His presence. David
described it this way.

> You have said, "Seek My face [inquire for and require
> My presence as your vital need].' My heart says to You,
> 'Your face (Your presence), Lord, will I seek, inquire
> for, and require [of necessity and on the authority of
> Your Word]."
>
> Psalm 27:8 AMP

Seeking God's face is all about being in His presence. That is where His glory shines on us. That is God's desire for His covenant people. That is why He commands the high priest to cover His people with the following blessings.

> 'The LORD bless you and keep you;
>> the LORD makes <u>his face shine</u> upon you
>>> and be gracious to you;
>> the LORD <u>turns his face</u> toward you
>>> and give you peace."
>>>> Numbers 6:24-26, emphasis added

In His presence when His face shines on us, His glory covers us. Since He dwells in an unapproachable glorious light of holiness, beauty, power, strength, and majesty; we receive an impartation that will change us from glory to glory into His likeness. The God of Jacob, among other things, is the God of prophetic destiny for His people.

Challenges Bring Our Prophetic Destiny into Light

A person can't have true rest until the realization of what God created him or her to accomplish is brought to light. God reveals His prophetic destiny to individuals in different ways and at different stages of life, but everyone is born with a prophetic destiny, like Jacob. That is one of the reasons why the Bible says, "Seeking the God of Jacob," rather than the God of Abraham or Isaac. We know that the name "God of ɔfers to the God of covenant. Abraham is the one who

ɔvenant and walked with God. He is also called the "God

of Isaac," which can mean the God of promises or blessings. Abraham received the covenant, and Isaac received the blessings of the covenant. Jacob, on the other hand, received his prophetic destiny and later entered into the full revelation of his prophetic destiny for future blessings. What God promised both Abraham and Isaac were fully realized in the life of Jacob. The nation of covenant is called by his prophetic name, Israel, which was a picture of new identity.

Seeking the God of Jacob, among other things, is seeking his prophetic destiny without giving up because of challenges along the way. The starting point in fulfilling that destiny is to hear clearly what God has said or even is saying now. The call of God is unchangeable. God doesn't change His mind about our destiny since He created us for that purpose. In fact, He called us by our God-given names and honored us as individuals before we were born (Isaiah 40:1-5).

The word given by God, or the promises or call of God, is your weapon to fight against everything that tries to stop you from reaching your destiny. We usually refer to this as hearing the call of God. Once we receive a revelation of God's plan for our lives and embrace that plan, we are on our way. In some cases, the Lord places that destiny in a person which becomes like a burning fire within that person. For some, God gives a burden or a care for things related to their destiny, which makes them restless. God uses that to guide an individual to his or her destiny, like Jacob.

For Moses the burden was for His people. He was willing to

give up everything: title, pleasure, opportunities, and fame because of the fire of destiny in his life. Although Moses did not have a direct encounter with God until he was 80-years old, he was driven by the prophetic destiny that was in him. On the other hand, Jeremiah heard from the Lord about his prophetic destiny when he was young and was encouraged by the Lord to embrace his purpose. David was told about his prophetic destiny and anointed when he was young.

The Lord has revealed to individuals their prophetic destiny in different ways and manners in biblical days as well as down through history, and it continues today. William Wilberforce, a British statesman and reformer, knew his prophetic destiny was to abolish the brutal British slave trade. In the late 1700s and early 1800s, Wilberforce fought and won a heroic 20-year battle against slavery that changed history. President Abraham Lincoln was inspired when he read about Wilberforce's perseverance. Lincoln later led the United States through the Civil War that ended in preserving the Union and abolishing slavery in our nation. Lincoln's destiny was fulfilled at the cost of his own life near the end of the war. President Lincoln was a humble man of God who was often maligned and misunderstood for his moral standards and determination to free a race of people and a nation.

Paying the Price

In the more modern times of the 21st century, best-selling author, Eric Metaxas, who wrote the book *Amazing Grace* tells the story of William Wilberforce's battle against slavery. He also released a book entitled, *Bonhoeffer: Pastor, Martyr, Prophet, Spy*. This brilliant biography of

Dietrich Bonhoeffer reveals a man who truly sought God's face and demonstrated a level of courage and faith that surpasses mankind's humanity in the face of the monstrous evil perpetrated by Adolph Hitler and his Nazi regime. Dietrich was safe in the United States but chose to return to Germany to stand firmly with the persecuted church. He did everything in his power to smuggle Jews into neutral Switzerland and even participated in plans to overthrow the Nazi regime. One book endorser wrote, "Bonhoeffer was a clear-headed, convicted Christian who submitted to no one and nothing except God and His Word."

Bonhoeffer was executed by Hitler's direct order on April 7, 1945 just two weeks before the Allied forces liberated the camp where his hanging took place. Through it all, he sought God and found Him. A German doctor who witnessed Bonhoeffer's death later wrote,

> Through the half-open door to one room of the huts,
> I saw Pastor Bonhoeffer kneeling on the floor praying
> fervently to his God. I was most deeply moved by the
> way this lovable man prayed, so devout and so certain
> that God heard his prayer.... In the almost fifty years
> as a doctor, I have hardly ever seen a man die so
> entirely submissive to the will of God.

We each have a prophetic destiny that God has ordained for us. We simply must seek God fervently and allow Him to lead us one step at a time into our calling and purpose in His timing. We may not be called to as dramatic a prophetic destiny as Wilberforce or Bonhoeffer, but

God's purpose for you and for me is equally important in His eyes. Each person has a different calling, and we should not compare with others. Look at others for encouragement.

Challenges are part of the package of a destiny ordained by God. The life of Joseph is a very good example for this. Joseph had a dream about his prophetic destiny when he was a youth. But it took him a long, very hard and difficult journey to reach his prophetic destiny. In the meantime, on that journey both his prophetic destiny dream and personal character were tested. He was a hardworking, trustworthy person. The Lord blessed the work of his hands. "The LORD was with Joseph and he prospered, and he lived in the house of his Egyptian master. When his master saw that the LORD was with him and that the LORD gave him success in everything he did" (Genesis 39:2-3). In comparison, my challenges are much easier and normal. When I was going through my challenges, they were genuine.

If You Go to Church...

Going back to my story after I passed the challenge of hard working, a test of faith came. I was in eighth grade. My grade was excellent. I started Bible studies for students in the public school that met once a week during lunch hour. One Sunday afternoon when I came back from church, the wife of my Indian teacher was waiting for me. I greeted her before I went into my room. She asked me where I came from. I told her I was coming from church. She said, "If you go to church, you can't stay here. If you go to church next Sunday, don't come back. But if you stop going to church, you can stay." I was shocked. I said to her, "You know my parents can't support me in school, but I chose the Lord." She said, "You have a week to make your final decision."

On Monday morning, I went to school thinking this is my last week of school and my future hope about education. It was one of the hardest days of my life. After the first period, the room teacher asked me to stay behind during the break. He said, "I have a very good news for you. Your grade is the highest in school. You are qualified to go to Addis Ababa and compete for the General Wingate scholarship." I said, "No, thank you. I don't want to go." He was surprised. He didn't expect that type of response. He insisted on finding out what was going on in my life. Finally, I told him that it is my last week in school, and I didn't know where I would be next week since I didn't have a place to stay. He said, "Okay, I will get back to you and left." On Thursday morning during break time, he came and told me to go and get my things from the Indian home during lunch time. I said to him, "Sir, where do I go?" He told me that he talked with two American teachers who would like to give a room and also pay you for taking care of their horses. That was just great for me, since I grew up on a farm where the major means of transportation was riding horses. I felt at home.

I moved that afternoon into the room they had prepared for me. It was much a better room with no working at night or after school. Sunday morning one of the teachers knocked at my door and said, "I heard you like to go church on Sundays. Here is my bicycle, please feel free to ride to church. This is the same Sunday the Indian lady told me that I could not to go church, and if went, I wouldn't have place to stay.

I was able to take the national exam for secondary school that school year and passed with very good results. I continued my high school in Gerasu Duki High School through ninth grade.

In spite of all the challenges of school and faith, the hand of God and His provision has always been with me. The joy of the Lord has been my strength at every turn of my journey. For me, that is the true sign of proper prosperity. The Lord providing for my needs to fulfill His purpose.

CHAPTER 6

EMBRACING PROPHETIC DESTINY

Ninth grade was one of my best school year. I had a place to stay and very bright Christian friends. We were outstanding in our studies and had developed a healthy competition. Each person was trying to become first every semester. Because of that, I started dreaming about the possibility of going into the medical field to become a medical doctor. I wanted to be free from poverty and help my parents who were aging. In other words, I was dreaming about breakout from my situation and going into breakthrough. Year after year, God faithfully took care of my needs so I could continue my education. Though I dreamed of becoming a medical doctor, God had other ideas. In other words, I wanted to go to medical school to become rich and wealthy. I completed ninth grade with excellent grades.

After school ended for the summer break, my American teachers went home for their summer vacation, but they didn't give me any support for summer. They told me before they left I could do whatever I wanted during the summer break. I decided to stay in town instead of going home and help my father on the farm, as I typically did. On Sunday at church my spiritual mother, who led me to the Lord and discipled me, asked what my plans were for the summer. After she heard my plans, she said, "I have something you might like to do this summer for about a month." When I asked her, she told me there was a special summer Bible school in Addis Ababa. She would like to sponsor me, if I would attend. She also told me that one of my best friends would be there. I said, "Okay!" She made the arrangements, and I went to Addis for the summer. I was excited about spending the summer in the capital city of Ethiopia and studying the Bible.

Willingness to Obey His Will

When I arrived and started classes, I was enjoying it. One teacher was Peter Cottrell, a missionary from London, England. He taught the Epistle of Romans. He was a very good teacher, and I looked forward to his class every day. One day he decided to read Daniel 12:3, for no obvious reason, before he started teaching Romans. He read,

> Those who are wise will shine like the brightness of the heavens, and those who lead many to righteousness, like the stars for ever and ever.
>
> Daniel 12:3

He didn't tell us why he read the verse, nor did he explain the meaning of the verse and how it related to the study of the Book of Romans. I believe, from conversation with him later, he didn't even know why he had read it. But I discovered the reason that night.

When he read the verse, I felt what the Jewish people felt on the day of Pentecost after Peter spoke, "When the people heard this, they were cut to the heart and said to Peter and the other apostles, 'Brothers, what shall we do?'" (Acts 2:37). That was exactly how I felt during the class. After class, I tried to forget that verse and continue with my studies. But that was a worthless effort. I didn't know how to take out that sword from my heart. After the class reading, all I was hearing was, *I would like for you to go to Bible school to prepare yourself to lead my people to righteousness.* I didn't like that voice. I tried to resist it with everything that was in me.

I understood God's plan was for me to go to Bible school. I fought not only against the idea of going to Bible school, but also against God. I made a list of all the reasons why Bible school was a bad choice for me. For one, I was trying to rebuild my relationship with my parents and desired to support myself and my family. I told myself the proper way to prosper is not by going to Bible school and living on handouts the rest of my life. I was miserable for three days. Unable to sleep, I got up during the night and woke up a friend to pray with me. I was wrestling with God, but God is the winner. He knows our heart and His power gives us the strength to overcome. At this time, getting to that place of breakout for breakthrough was not easy. I prayed a simple prayer, "Lord, wherever you want me to go, I will go. But please give me your peace about it."

The journey for prophetic destiny takes us to the place where we have to make a choice between the will of God and our own will and plans. This is the case for everyone who is committed to God's will. The Lord Jesus underscored the importance of this when He said, "I have food to eat that you know nothing about" (John 4:32). He also said before the cross, "Father, if you are willing, take this cup from me; yet not my will, but yours be done" (Luke 22:42). That means without a total surrender to the purpose and will of God, it is impossible to reach our prophetic destiny. That was what the Lord showed me through the encounter I had during summer Bible school. The decision I made that night became the foundation for my God-ordained journey, and it continues today.

Preparation to Fulfill My Prophetic Destiny

After I submitted to the will of God, I knew that I should change my life course and go to Bible school to prepare myself to obey my calling. The following week, I talked with the same teacher. He told me about Grace Bible Institute (GBI) in Jimma province. He also informed me that GBI only accepts students who have completed high school, or have a college degree. He said I could fill an application and see what the school recommends, and he would give me an application form. Since I didn't want to stop my high school education and go to Bible school, the information pleased me very much. I took the application, filled it out and returned to him to send it in the hope that the Bible school would reject me on a qualification basis since I hadn't completed high school.

After two weeks the school sent me their new admission policy. The new admission policy beginning that academic year required that the school accept students who are able to pass the school admittance exam. It encouraged every student to come prepared to take the exam and pay school tuition in order to finalize the admission process. That was good news, because I would not pass the test that was prepared for college level students. I didn't have a high school completion certificate, and I certainly didn't have money for the tuition.

The rest of my summer was a real wrestling experience, to say the least. When I told my parents I applied to go to Bible school, my father was furious. He said, "It is one thing to accept that religion, but now you are going to be a priest for that religion!" All my school friends were dismayed at my decision. One of my teachers thought I was quitting school because of financial problems. He looked for me and came to discourage me from going to Bible school. He promised he would support me by covering all my expenses in high school. I had to say, "No, thank you." Some of my close friends felt I was losing my mind. As hard as it was, the summer came to an end.

I didn't have money for clothes, transportation, school tuition, and all the other necessary things. I was leaving for Jimma to take the entrance exam on Tuesday, but I didn't have money. On Sunday, I went by my small country church. I was asked to give a testimony about my call to Bible school and say goodbye. The offering time came before I was invited to the pulpit. The only thing I had was $0.25, I heard the Holy Spirit saying give it as an offering. I struggled; I didn't want to give that $0.25. Finally, I threw it into the offering.

I gave my testimony and shared about the Bible school in a few words. After the church service, a missionary kid, who was my age, came to say goodbye and gave me an envelope with money in it. I asked him what it was. He said he worked for his parents all summer and earned this money. That morning the Lord told him to give it to me, all of it. I said to him, "Are you sure?" He answered with joy on his face, "I am very sure." He said, "Have a mercy journey to Jimma on Tuesday." And he left to go back to school in Addis Ababa.

The next day, I bought some clothes, had a haircut and purchased a bus ticket to Jimma. I was still planning to return to continue in high school. I arrived at GBI and was greeted by the school director, Mr. Ted Veer. The following day was the entrance exam. He corrected the test the same day and told us the results. He called first a person with highest score and congratulated him. Then he called my name and said my score was the second highest. He welcomed me to school, "The other good news for you somebody came this week and paid your tuition for three years." That day I embraced my prophetic destiny fully. I stopped fighting the Lord's plan for my life and made peace with myself.

The Lord started sharpening my spiritual gifts, particularly, in the area of teaching and preaching. Students were assigned to various churches in the surrounding cities every Sunday. I started preaching and ministering every Sunday which I enjoyed very much.

When I was a senior, I was selected from the student body to go to another province, Yirga Chefe, Sidamo, to speak at an important annual conference. I faced two major challenges. I had not spoken at a large gathering with some well-known speakers, both national and international. The second challenge was I didn't have proper clothes for the occasion. I arrived at the conference, and they put me in a missionary home. According to the conference schedule, I was the first speaker. It was an open-air meeting with a large amount of people. The missionary wife was waiting for me to change before the program. But the only clothes I had was the ones that I was wearing. Finally, she figured out before long what was happening. She brought me her husband's white shirt. Her husband was very tall and big. I was 5'8" and very thin. I put it on, pulled it back and held it with my left hand. I used my right hand to hold my Bible. I preached that way for three days. The Lord moved mightily in that conference, and I still remember my message in 1972. To this day, I also have that Bible.

I graduated from GBI in 1972 and moved to Addis Ababa to work at a youth center on weekends and teach Bible classes at Grace Christian Academy during the week. The Lord opened the door for me to attend high school to earn my high school certificate in order to apply for college while I was teaching Bible classes in the same school. It was a wonderful, fruitful year as the Lord blessed the work of my hands both in teaching Bible classes in the high school and working with the university students on the weekends at the youth center. Every weekend I witnessed students coming to the Lord. That year reminds me of Joseph's time in Potiphar's house when everything he touched was blessed before the biggest challenge of his life.

The LORD blessed the Egyptian's house because of

Joseph. The LORD's blessing was on all that he owned, in his house and in his fields.

Genesis 39:5

Like Joseph, a challenging season also came for me in 1974 when the socialist movement overthrew Emperor Haile Selassie. The military took over the government. High schools and universities were closed. The communists took senior high school students and university students into the countryside to teach farmers literacy and socialism doctrines. I was among them. The 125 students in my group chose me to be their leader. We were stationed in a town called Gambela, close to the Sudan border, for two years. This was where my faith was tested further.

I was pressured to deny my faith and join them in communist propaganda and doctrine. Some of the students who were committed to the communism philosophy felt I was a hindrance to their agenda. With the leadership of a few radical students, they decided to get rid of me by mobilizing the student body against me. That didn't work as they planned. One night they gathered around me, put me on stage and surrounded me to take action. They asked me to stop talking about Jesus and join the revolution. I told them gently, but firmly, that they should give up on communism and join me in following Jesus Christ our Savior. At that point, they split into two groups. The group opposing me and those that started supporting me. They started fighting each other. I stepped into their midst to break the fight.

I found a church without a pastor and began spending my evenings preaching the Gospel, even though I was working for the Communist Party daily. The communists recognized my lack of fervor for their doctrines and clear preference for Christianity. In those days, communists didn't fire teachers like me. They usually killed us.

I was no exception. Three times, they came while I was preaching and lined up to kill me, on Sundays. But each time, they fell away, fighting among themselves. One of the men in this group slept in my dorm. For six weeks, he carried a knife with him every night to kill me, but God protected me.

Afterward, a number of those guys came to the Lord after their leader became blind suddenly and left for Addis Ababa overnight.

I continued on with my ministry as pastor of the local church and working with local farmers. In that challenging situation, the Holy Spirit started speaking to me about writing a book. I never wrote anything previously except a graduation paper for Bible school. I didn't have an interest in writing.

Out of obedience to the voice of God, I started writing my first book, *Christ in The Tabernacle,* while I was pastoring a church left by missionaries because of persecution. After two years of serving as pastor, the time came for us to return to the capital city. That book was published by SIM Press in 1980, after I left the country. The book, published in Amharic, continues in circulation and is popular today. The Amharic language is the national language in Ethiopia. I went back to work with the youth center in Addis Ababa, Ethiopia. We changed it to a local church and named it Fellowship Church. I became the first full-time minister at Fellowship Church.

I went to night school to finish my high school education to receive a completion certificate. I went on to take my university entrance national exam in 1978.

CHAPTER 7

KEEPING PASSION ALIVE FOR PROPHETIC DESTINY

The Lord uses situations, people, political and social systems to mature us so that we are able to advance with our prophetic destiny. Numerous great examples are found throughout the Bible as well as on pages of history books. In the Bible, Joseph is one of the more significant examples. The Lord used his brothers, Potiphar's wife and a time in prison to mature him for his prophetic destiny. The Lord showed him his prophetic destiny while he was a youth. After that, He took him on a life journey to prepare and qualify him for a leadership role in Egypt, which was his prophetic destiny.

Moses was another person whose prophetic destiny was prescribed beforehand. He was taken on a long, 80 years of life journey before reaching his purpose, prophet of destiny, to set the people of God free.

King David, a man who was after God's own heart, also went through a similar journey. In the case of David, the Lord used Saul, the

King of Israel, to develop David to become one of the best kings and a shepherd in Jewish history.

When we are committed to His purpose, which is our prophetic destiny, God uses everything to help us achieve that goal.

> We know that in all things God works for the good of
> those who love him, who have been called according
> to his purpose.
>
> Romans 8:28

The common thing to all the above and to everyone who has reached their prophetic destiny with determination is their ability to keep the passion and fire alive. Every challenge we face on the journey of prophetic destiny aims to put out our fire.

I started my life journey with passion to learn how to read and write. When I accepted the Lord Jesus as my personal Savior, my passion for God and doing His will became a driving force in my life. I had passion for two things more than anything else; the glory of God and higher education. Even after I graduated from Bible school and completed my high school, I started serving the Lord fulltime with my passion for the greater glory of God, and then further education.

Don't You Know That We Are in Revolution?

After I came back from the Development Campaign, as the socialist party called it, my ministry accelerated with great speed. I started seeing the impact of my ministry, particularly on the youth. In the meantime, in 1976 the persecution against Christians had become extremely severe. The Lord protected me so many times during those days. I came very close to being killed many, many times. Once after they put a gun on my chest, the commander told him to let me go. Another time they missed me by a second and killed a couple.

However, I didn't have any fear. Every Sunday, the revolution guards would close our community to stop us from having church or going out to church. I would dress in my finest clothing and carry my Bible in hand and go ask them to let me leave the neighborhood. When they asked me where I was going, I told them exactly where I would be speaking or preaching. They let me leave every Sunday.

In 1978, I received a letter from the socialist party that asked me about my contribution to the society besides preaching. Since that was their standard procedure before they captured a person and sent them to prison, my friends and church leaders urged me to leave the country rather than spending the rest my life in prison. They said I was too young to die in prison, but if I went immediately, I might be helpful in the future to churches from outside the nation. It was nearly impossible to obtain a visa to leave the country legally. I told the church leaders and my friends, if, in fact, leaving the country is the will of God for me, the Lord would open the door for me to leave the country legally. At the same time, SIM offered me a scholarship to go Bible school in Nigeria.

I accepted that and went to the immigration office to ask for an exit visa. At that time, this was unthinkable. Everybody was terrified by the person who was in charge of the exit visa department. I waited for my turn and went in. He asked me what I wanted. I said, "Sir, I would like to get an exit visa to go Bible school." When he heard that, with a great surprise on his face, he looked at me and asked, "What did you just say?" I responded, "I would like to obtain an exit visa to go to Bible school." "Don't you know we are in revolution? Don't you know we are the middle of a revolution? You are asking me to give you an exit visa?" I said, "Yes, sir. I am committed to the study of the Bible as much you are committed to socialism." He looked at me again and said come back after eight days. I said, "Thank you and left."

When I shared this with my friends and church leaders, they panicked. They were absolutely sure that he would put me in prison that day. Some asked me not to go back for the appointment. I told them that since I had given him my word, I would go back. I showed up according to my appointment. He looked at me and asked if I was the one who requested an exit visa to go to Bible school. I said, "Yes, sir!" He said, "Have you changed your mind?" I responded by saying, "No, I haven't." He wrote the exit visa to be given to me, with priority. I obtained my visa and left the country within two days' time.

I left for Kenya to go to Nigeria for Bible school in August 1978. A missionary who came to pick me up at Nairobi airport asked me why I wanted to go to Nigeria. I told him SIM had given me a scholarship. He explained the cultural challenges I would face in West Africa. He told me about another Bible school very close to Nairobi, a place call Machakos. He told me if I would go there, I could talk with a SIM person since he has authority. I told him that I would like to go to Machakos, Kenya. The next day he took me there and explained to the school director my situation. I was accepted the same day and started class the next day. I attended the school for a quarter.

The standard of the school was very similar to what I had in Ethiopia. Because of that, I didn't want to continue in the same school. I started looking for possibilities. I applied for Biola University in California among other higher education institutions. At the end of the quarter, I made a decision that if I didn't hear from one of the universities, I would go back to Ethiopia.

We Should Admit Him

Biola University accepted me for the fall of 1979 and wrote a letter of admission to come the following year. I was waiting for that letter before returning to Ethiopia. After the admission department's secretary mailed the letter, she became miserable. She didn't know why. She went to the director of admission and told him. The director called a special meeting and asked her what they should do. She told them, "We should admit him as a special student for spring semester." Though they had not done that before, they agreed to do just that. She wrote a second letter and invited me to join them for the January class. The first letter she sent was delayed and the second letter came first. By the time the first letter arrived, I had already completed the immigration process. The lady who was at the American Embassy would send it back to Ethiopia to request a visa from Ethiopia. The day I went for my visa, she was gone for vacation. The person who was in charge gave my visa and told me that he knew about Biola University and wished me the best.

I arrived on January 24, 1979 in America to study at the Bible Institute of Los Angeles, Biola University. Subsequently, I earned my undergraduate degree at Biola in Intercultural Studies, including Cultural Anthropology and Cross-Cultural Communication.

Either You Are Very Smart or Stupid!

SIM gave me a scholarship for four years. Because of my passion for higher education, I made a decision to study hard and try earning BA and MA degrees in four years. I graduated at the end December 1980. I planned to go to seminary for graduate school. I was accepted in seminaries; however, I wanted to stay around Biola and attend Talbot Seminary. One Sunday after church, I was disturbed. I didn't know what was going on. I started praying. I knew it was about my future. That week I heard the Lord saying, "Going to seminary is not my plan for you." I was shocked. He made it clear that His plan for me was to continue with higher education. I started looking for a university where I could look into the role of an education in resource development. A friend of mine told me that I should consider Michigan State University (MSU).

Amazing but that same week, Dr. Ted Ward came to speak at Talbot Seminary. When I heard about it, I went to see him. I told him who I am and my desire to go MSU. He looked at me and said, "Either you are very smart or very stupid!" I said to him maybe the later one, but I definitely wanted to attend MSU. He was in the education department. He told me that as an international student, I needed to be accepted six months in advance. I told him that since I don't have six months, I would like his assistance in sending me an application.

We Don't Know You!

I filled the application and sent it to MSU, but I didn't hear from the university. I went to Lansing, Michigan the beginning of 1981 to start class on January 5. I went to the admission office to find out what was happening. The admission department said, "We don't know you. There is no record of you, and we can't do anything for you." I showed them the copy of my application. I was told even if we accept today, the State law requirement is six months for international students. I don't have six months. I am here, and I am not going anywhere. They waived the state law to admit me. I started classes for my MA in Curriculum Design and Community Development.

Your Scholarship Is for a BA

The scholarship was for four years when I came to the USA as a student. My desire was that in those four years to go as far as I could go before returning to Ethiopia. When I completed my BA in two years, I was asked to go back to Ethiopia. But with SIM, I had two more years, and I wanted to get my MA. After much discussion, they agreed, and I went to MSU for my MA. However, because of passion for education, I worked hard and completed my MA in less than a year and started my Ph.D. I went back to SIM and told them I still have one more year, and I would like to start my Ph.D. They said, "Your scholarship is for a BA." I told them that I signed an agreement for four years, and I still have one more year.

I gave them two choices. The first choice was to honor the four-year agreement and pay my school tuition, and after a year return to Ethiopia and work for them. The second choice was to release me from the agreement to be on my own. They agreed to free me from any obligation. They did it with their blessings. I became a free man without any money! Yes, total obedience wholeheartedly to receive the revealed will of God is the proper way to prosper. I had a breakout for breakthrough into the next steps for my prophetic destiny. I felt that day I was the richest person on Earth, because of my commitment to the will of God. The foundation of lasting blessings is to make the will and purposes of God our priority for the provision to be released as it is written.

> Seek first his kingdom and his righteousness, and all
> these things will be given to you as well.
>
> Matthew 6:33

In addition to our commitment to the will and purpose of God, we should keep the passion of God within us alive. We do this by having a different spirit like Caleb, who was blessed for his obedience. Having a different spirit enables us to stand firm in the face of challenges in obedience to the will of God wholeheartedly and keep the passion for Him which is an entry way to lasting blessings (Deuteronomy 28:1-11).

I Just Came to Be with You

The only way we keep the passion and love for God alive during challenging situations is to stay close to Him. When my daughter Keah was a little girl, she would come into my prayer room early in the mornings when I was praying. I don't know how she sensed it, but no matter what time I woke up, she came into my prayer room. Usually I asked her, "Shall I take you to your bedroom? It is too early for you to wake up. How about going to our bedroom so that you can sleep with Mom in our bed?" Her answer was always, the same, "No, Ababa. I just want to be with you." One day the Holy Spirit said to me, "When is the last time you came just to be with me?" That day my understanding of prayer was changed. Since then, I go to prayer to seek His presence more than answers to my questions.

CHAPTER 8

FOLLOWING HIS LEADING FOR PROPHETIC DESTINY

The one who calls you is faithful and he will do it.

1 Thessalonians 5:24

"Yes, you are free from any obligation to SIM!" This statement was exciting and liberating as I looked forward to my calling and the future. But when I looked at my circumstances, it was very terrifying. At that stage I went back to the Lord in prayer to ask Him what I should do. I didn't have any money or support. I didn't have a work permit either. I didn't know where to go from this point.

I felt like Jacob, who had a prophetic destiny. But in the wilderness, he tried to sleep on a pillow of rock. Yes, he had passion and commitment to enter into what the Lord spoke about him before his birth, but he didn't know how. He found himself running away from his brother who was trying kill him. He had nothing in this unexpected place. That was me after I completed my MA and was released from obligation to SIM. The beauty of Jacob's story is that in this hopeless place, he had a divine encounter and received clear direction and promise from the Lord. He had heard God's voice for himself and experienced the presence of God for the first time. After that great encounter, the Lord said, "I will not leave you until I have done what I have promised you" (Genesis 28:15). That promise led Jacob and continues to protect the Israelites even until today.

The Lord reminded me that day about His promise to me. I heard the Lord clearly saying, "Continue with your education. I will fulfil what I have promised." But I didn't know where to start since I didn't have anything. I went to Professor Ted Ward and shared with him my situation. He was excited about my decision. He really liked me at the first encounter. He had seen the hand of the Lord on my life. He started raising funds for my education right way.

My immediate challenge was to obtain a student visa to stay. To do that, I would have to be admitted for the Ph.D. program. I went to the international student office for an admission form. The lady in charge asked me for proof of scholarship. I told her that I didn't have a scholarship. She asked, "Do you have money in your bank account?" My answer was, "No!" "Do you have a work study promise from the education department or Natural Resources Development?" Again, my answer was, "No!" She looked at me, "You are wasting my time, and I don't want to see you here again. Get out!" I heard that previously from my high school director, and I was not surprised or disturbed. I left her office and started praying as I was walking toward my dorm. I stopped at my mailbox. I saw a letter mailed from

California. When I opened it, it was a check for $1000 with a hand-written note, "Use it for the glory of God. You don't need to know the sender." I was so excited and went back to the International Student Office and showed her the check. She didn't believe me!

The breakthrough started with that check. I earned a graduate study fellowship from Urban Development Department the same week. I registered for fall classes. I was also hired by the Office for International Networks in Education and Development (INET). I continued studies as I was working and ministering at the same time. God also allowed me to provide leadership for the exiled Ethiopian Church worldwide. I served as Executive Director for Ethiopian Evangelical Students Association (EESA) for many years. Among other things, I organized annual conferences for EESA in Chicago every summer. I helped Bible study groups become local churches as well as planting Ethiopian churches among Ethiopian communities. God placed a growing burden in my heart for emerging leaders.

I continued my studies at MSU in Curriculum Design and Community Development. Curriculum and Non-Formal Education included a role in the education development, curriculum for staff development, leadership training, adult education, and curriculum research under Professor Ted Ward. My minor was Community Development, including concepts and principles of community development, field techniques in community development, and international development.

After completing my class work, I decided to do field research for my dissertation. The research focused on Core Curriculum for

Field Staff Training for Development. This included a case study in East Africa with one nonprofit community development organization. For about seven months, I was stationed in Kenya and carried out field research in six East African countries. During the field research, I was engaged in two things simultaneously. One was providing the organization feedback on their work and the training of change agents. The second was planting and pastoring an Ethiopian church among Ethiopian refugees in Nairobi. The Lord gave great favor and success in doing both, completing my dissertation.

After the research, I returned to Lansing to finish my writing. I defended my work and earned my doctoral degree from MSU in Curriculum Design and Community Development in 1985.

Until my graduation, the Lord had directed me step by step in very amazing ways. As I shared at the beginning of the chapter, I started the doctoral program without money, but the day I graduated I had $10,000 in my savings. When I was in Bible school in Ethiopia and before I finished high school, I had told a close friend that one day I would earn my doctorate and serve the Lord. He looked at me and said, "It's a good thing to have a dream." When I invited that friend for my graduation, he said, "The Lord has done amazing things for me, but your life is unreal."

After graduation in 1985 with the Ph.D., the question was, "What now?" I was ready to go into full-time Christian ministry. I just want to know where and how. I received an offer from two nonprofit organizations. I sought the Lord about it, but He didn't give a green light for either of them.

After my graduation, Professor Ted Ward announced his retirement. The College of Education started looking for his replacement. The following week one of the professors I had worked for as a research assistance called me into his office. He told me the College of Education would like to hire me to replace Professor Ted Ward. That was a big surprise and a shock for me. I didn't believe that was from the Lord. I told him that I couldn't accept the office unless the college would hire me as an assistant professor. I don't want to start as a lecturer. The word that came out of his mouth was, "That is impossible!" I said okay and left his office feeling foolish.

After two days the same person contacted me, "To my surprise, the dean of college of education agreed to hire you as an assistant professor." I joined MSU, College of Education, as an Assistant Professor, Adult and Continuing Education and as well as managing the Office for International Networks in Education and Development (INET). The Lord used my role to secure my green card. I worked for the university for three and half years.

I was blessed with a God-fearing wonderful woman of God. Genet and I met for the first time in Chicago at an Ethiopian Evangelical Association annual conference in the summer of 1983 and married in 1987. The details are in Chapter 10.

After we were married, one day as I was driving to our apartment from MSU, I heard the Lord saying, "Get ready! I will be moving you to your calling within six months." He didn't tell the place or the type of ministry. I came home and told Genet what I had heard. Telling her right away was not the right thing to do. Every day she kept asking if I heard anything else. Sure enough, in the fifth month, I received a call from Compassion International (CI). After a few days, Genet and I flew to Colorado Springs for a job interview. The amazing part of this was that I had met Dr. Wess Stafford in the first class I took while at MSU. At the beginning of the class, the professor asked us to introduce ourselves to the class. I introduced myself as an evangelist from Ethiopia. My boldness in introducing myself as an evangelist in a major public university surprised Wess. He looked for me during break and introduced himself as a fellow African. I looked at him and said, "You don't look like an African." He said, "It is only my color; otherwise, I am a true African. I grew up as a missionary kid in West Africa, and all my friends and values are from Africa." We became not only very close friends, but also covenant brothers for life. We started weekly Bible studies and prayer meetings. The rest is history. When Wess introduced me to his mother, he said, "Mom, Alemu is my true brother, although he didn't come from your womb. The only difference between us is our skin color."

Wess was sent to MSU to study for a Ph.D. as a part of his preparation to become the next president of CI. He was the one who introduced me to CI ministries. CI is a Christian humanitarian aid organization with a child sponsorship program dedicated to the long-term development of children living in poverty. When I worked for CI both as an employee and consultant, I traveled to many countries where CI had a national office. During those times, I witnessed the protection of God on my journeys, over and over again. Here are a few examples. I went to Bunia in the Democratic Republic of the Congo and conducted a leadership workshop for pastors who partner with CI in children's ministry. The training workshop was for three days. I conducted the training the first day, and it was powerful. The pastors, bishops and church leaders responded very well. I was very excited about the remaining two days. However, that night the Lord said you have to leave the city tomorrow. I said, "Lord, why? How I do I justify leaving in the middle of the worship? These are leaders who would make a great difference for this poor nation." The Lord didn't answer my question, and He simply said, "Leave this town tomorrow." I prayed most of the night and made a decision to talk to the national director for the CI work. At breakfast, I shared with the director with great fear and respect. He responded by saying, "I have known you for many years. I believe you and let me call the mission aviation, the only means of transportation out of the town. After breakfast while I was waiting for him, I started the workshop. He came back from talking to the guy who was in charge of mission aviation and interrupted the workshop and said, "I have good news for Dr. Alemu. There is a flight today, and they have one seat left. I have secured that for you. Go and get ready. I apologized to the leaders and left. That was the last flight from the town for a long time!

The town had been attracted by my liberation and closed the mission aviation! Yes, on the journey of our prophetic destiny, God doesn't only provide but also protects.

Once, we were stopped by a liberation group called FLMN in Colombia for hours, and finally for an unknown reason they let us go. But I know the reason. It was the Lord's protection! I guess partially it is my color skin, but I have been put in a dark room and waited many times in Colombia, Peru and Quito, Ecuador. I would sit, read and pray. After I take authority over the enemy, they usually come and say, "You can go."

In 1989, I accepted the position of Senior Leadership Development Specialist with CI and moved from Lansing, MI to Colorado Springs, CO. I was hired as an education specialist to help with school curriculum in schools supported by CI. Before long, I was promoted to senior leadership development position. I provided leadership training for the CI staff worldwide as well as leading partners' development leadership training workshops through CI offices in many nations. I worked with CI as full-time staff for 11 years and as an outside consultant for more than a decade.

In addition, in 1989 I planted the Evangelical Ethiopian Church in Denver and served as senior pastor for about nine years. God has continually expanded my vision, and He continues to lead me through this amazing journey of my prophetic destiny. Today, I train pastors, businesspeople and politicians in nations on six continents. I encourage them to make the most of God's call on their lives in strategic parts of the world through the ministry of Gospel of Glory. Nothing about me is imposing. Nothing in my background hinted that God would have me doing what I am doing today to change history.

Ababa, Hush!

For me, ministry is not what I do for God, but my daily commitment to listen to His heart, and let God be in me and through me. In the morning when I pray, my son would come from time to time and stretch his hands as a sign of pick me up. My typical response was to pick him up and walk and pray. One day he did something very usual, most of the time he leaned on my chest until I finished my prayer. That day he said, "Ababa, Hush!" I was surprised and since he was a very serious child, I continued praying in silence. After a while he said, "Ababa, now you can pray out loud." I wondered and asked him, "Why did ask me to hush!" He said, "Because I was trying to listen to your heart, and when you prayed out loud, I was not able hear your heart." Since that day, my focus has been to hush every noise to listen to His heart for my generation. All I do daily is trust His promise and follow His leading. Yes, He is faithful, and He does it for those who are determined to live in Him and for Him.

The one who calls you is faithful and he will do it.

1 Thessalonians 5:24

CHAPTER 9

COVENANT RELATIONSHIP FOR PROPHETIC DESTINY

For this reason, a man will leave his father and mother and be united to his wife, and they will become one flesh.

Genesis 2:24

Even I am surprised at how God took me from a truly remote farm in Ethiopia to school and three university degrees in the United States. But during this time, God has His biggest surprise by bringing me to another turning point on my journey. It was just like Genesis 1 and 2. God created Adam in His own image and gave him responsibilities from naming animals to ruling Earth and cultivate the garden. But He looked at Adam, "It is not good for the man to be alone. I will make a helper suitable for him" (Genesis 2:18). God realized that He should give him Eve.

"My name is Genet" (pronoun Ga-NET). Our God is the God of relationships. I would like Genet to tell her story. He created us to have a meaningful relationship with Him. "So, God created man in his own image, in the image of God he created him; male and female he created them. Then the man and his wife heard the sound of the LORD God as he was walking in the garden in the cool of the day" (Genesis 1:27, 3:8).

Jesus died on the cross to restore a fellowship that was broken because of sin. Through the price He paid with His life, He opened a door for anyone to have an everlasting fellowship with God. The invitation to that fellowship is for each one of us.

> We proclaim to you what we have seen and heard, so that you also may have fellowship with us. And our fellowship is with the Father and with his Son, Jesus Christ.
>
> 1 John 1:3

This is the basis for meaningful human relationships. God releases His blessings in the context of such relationships. "How good and pleasant it is when brothers live together in unity! For there the LORD bestows his blessing, even life forevermore" (Psalm 133:1,3).

Probably the most significant human relationship is the relationship between husband and wife. That is why starting with a right relationship, and keeping the right relationship in marriage and family, is so crucial. It's the foundation for other things in life. This is major part of the journey for our prophetic destiny.

God also demonstrates the importance of that relationship in His sight. Immediately after creating mankind in His image, God gave Adam a wife with whom to enjoy a union of complete vulnerability and love. God didn't give Adam and Eve the keys to the office or a bank account. He gave them one another as a gift to enjoy, in partnership for a lifetime of fellowship. The same continues for couples in covenant relationship today.

We need to notice God created two "banks" of relationship on each side of His river of blessing. There is the relationship we must have with God, and also the relationship with a loving husband or wife.

Relationship with God

The river of God's blessings for the family is based upon the relationship between husband and wife and their family. None of us dare ignore the importance of these covenant relationships, if we are on a journey of prophetic destiny!

Again, it is necessary to recognize the importance of starting points in life. This couple will enjoy the benefits of two of the most important relationships in life.

- The right relationship with God, and
- The right relationship in a marriage, the covenant that establishes a family.

Starting Right in a Marriage Relationship

To have a solid, ongoing relationship, it is important to start right. Therefore, it is very crucial to:

1. **Seek God's will first.**

    Knowing and fully accepting God's will is a solid foundation for everyone who would like to have a successful marriage, life, ministry, or business. God is faithful and reveals His purposes to those who are sincere. The Bible is full of God's promises to lead those who are committed to glorify Him in their ways and lifestyle.

2. **Obey God's will wholeheartedly.**

    God reveals His will to those who are determined to obey. The will of God is not "head knowledge" alone, but aimed at our hearts to give us the determination to follow Him. We must accept His will wholeheartedly. This, in turn, leads into a true, lasting commitment to enjoy His blessings.

3. **Commit to physical and mental purity.**

    In the process of waiting for the revealed will of God, it is necessary to stay pure, morally and sexually. It is particularly important to know you are not immune to temptation from pornography, compromising situations while dating, and the culture's emphasis on *anything goes* in terms of sexuality. In marriage, keeping this kind of purity is crucial for the health of the marriage covenant. Lack of purity in these areas destroys even the strongest of marriages. Remember this: even if you have failed, you need to allow God to restore you to purity. Here's how:

- Seek God.

- Ask for forgiveness.

- Avoid temptation.

- Find accountability with a prayer partner or small fellowship group.

- Determine to choose righteousness over sin when confronted with temptation.

4. Focus on true love.

One way of knowing God's perfect will is by having a true, genuine love for the opposite sex. The basis for a strong marriage is not physical attraction or infatuation, but a true love that will lead into a lasting commitment. Some of the characteristics of such love include:

- True care for the other person

- Genuine respect

- Self-sacrifice

- The ability to commit to a future together

5. **Check for the peace of God.**

The peace of God is more than a feeling of excitement. It's bigger than enjoying a physical attraction toward another person. It brings contentment, self-confidence and a true, lasting joy in companionship. God approves His perfect will by filling a seeker with His peace that is beyond logical human reasoning.

6. **Understand that God institutes marriage.**

7. **Marriage is more than a good idea that came out of human minds.**

    God established it, for His purposes. It was a part of God's perfect creation and in His design of perfection before sin entered the human picture. Marriage was established to illustrate God's covenant and love for His people. As such, it also illustrates and reflects the relationship between Christ and his Church. Christ honored marriage as He performed His first miracle in the context of marriage. It is a picture of a future and final hope (Revelation 19). It expresses God's purpose for today and the future. God institutes marriage to provide a solid foundation or basis for families, societies, communities, and nations. It is a school where individuals learn responsibility, self-sacrificing love, true submission, lasting commitment, covenant relationship, and selflessness. Best of all, marriage is the highly recommended graduate school of character development.

The foundation of the marriage I share with my wife, Genet, has been our relationship with God. God brought us together. God kept us, imperfect as we both were, for each other for years as we sought Him in prayer regarding everyday life.

The Starting Point of Two Becoming One

Genet's Story

The way the Lord brings two people together varies for every couple. Alemu and I were brought together in holy matrimony through a miracle of God. We met for the first time in Chicago at an Ethiopian church conference in the summer of 1983. I heard him speak during Christmas in Los Angeles that same year.

At the time we were both engaged to other people. (I believe that was God's protection over us.) His fiancée lived in Kenya, and my intended was in Ethiopia. We were both committed to our relationships, and because of our commitments, our focus was on college studies and God. Thus, we were not looking for relationships other than the relationships God gives us with brothers and sisters in Christ.

During this time, Alemu was living in Lansing, Michigan, and teaching at MSU. I lived in Fresno, California, and was attending Fresno Pacific College.

In 1985, the Lord began challenging me regarding my relationship with my fiancée. One day I called him in Ethiopia and asked him about his relationship with the Lord. He wasn't a Christian and had no interest in following Jesus. It broke my heart. I began praying more earnestly for his salvation, but he had no desire to know the Lord. At Christmas, the same year, I attended a three-day church conference in Los Angeles. My heart was heavy, and I asked the Lord why He wasn't changing my fiancée's heart. It was very difficult, as I knew I had to choose Jesus and end the engagement.

Alemu was a keynote speaker at the conference. The title of his message was, "Why are you struggling to remove the Glory of the Lord?" It was like BOOM! "Where does this guy get his sermon topics?" I asked myself.

Listening to the message, I asked the Lord, "Is it this ring that I've had a hard time removing? You have to help me, Lord!" I cried the entire time Alemu was preaching. But I made the decision to take off the engagement ring and obey God, rather than entangle my life with an unbeliever. This happened Christmas Eve morning in 1985.

The next day I made it a point to thank Alemu for obeying the Lord and giving us the message from God. Alemu told me he was engaged to an Eritrean Christian woman, but her parents opposed their relationship because of different ethnic backgrounds. (To this day, many Ethiopians and Eritreans are at odds. In fact, Eritrea recently split off from Ethiopia to become a separate country.) Alemu asked that I pray for him, and that God would change the heart of the girl's father. I returned to Fresno, and Alemu went back to Michigan.

Another year went by. I graduated from Fresno Pacific College in May 1986 and moved to Los Angeles. In December 1986, during Christmas, an annual conference was held at my church. Alemu is the guest speaker each year.

That year, Alemu's Christmas Eve subject was Jonah and the Ninevites. The message was very powerful and convicting to all Ethiopians and Eritreans in attendance. We were all crying. Alemu taught how Jonah didn't want the Ninevites to repent and be saved, because they were cruel toward the Israelites. Jonah was prejudiced and wanted them judged by God. The Ethiopians and Eritreans felt the same way toward each other.

You should understand that the Ethiopian-Eritrean issue is part of our story. I am Eritrean, too. My mother attended the 1986 conference, and the message challenged and convicted her. She was very prejudiced toward other ethnic groups in Ethiopia. Thus, she didn't want her children marrying anyone from a different ethnic group.

But God has an amazing sense of humor. While Alemu preached, my mother heard the Holy Spirit say, "This man will come to your house." Hearing this, she thought someone behind her was speaking, so she turned around to see who it was. However, no one was talking to her! Everyone was simply listening intently to the teaching. My mother thought, "Why would this man come to my house?" She had never met Alemu. The voice continued speaking. The third time the voice spoke, it also said, "I have given Genet to this man."

By then, my mother was very upset! She suspected that it might be the Lord talking to her, and she didn't like what He was saying! My mother was very angry as she left the church.

Knowing how Alemu's message would impact her, I talked to my mother that night to see how she was doing. Her eyes were red and puffy from crying. She was angry and irritated. I asked her what she thought of the message, and she said it was strong, but she knew she needed to hear it. But that wasn't all that was on her mind.

She asked, "Do you know the man?" I said, "Yes, his name is Alemu Beeftu. He's a great man of God."

"How well do you know him?" "I know he is a very respected man, Mommy."

She asked again, "How well do you know him?" This time, I heard the anger and resentment in her voice.

"Mommy, his teaching was not his word, but it was the Word of God. Don't be mad at him. Why are you angry at him?"

Then she said, "I'm not angry at him for teaching the Word of God, but I think he wants you!"

When she said that, I was shocked! I asked, "Did someone tell you that? Did Alemu tell you that? Did God tell you that?"

"No."

"Where did you get such an idea? If no one told you that, you shouldn't say such a thing! You can't tell anything like this to anyone!"

Mommy seemed relieved at that point. She agreed, thinking I wouldn't be interested in marrying Alemu.

But that isn't the message others had heard. That same evening, we returned to my sister's house where we were staying. When Alemu started speaking that night, my sister Regat heard the Lord say, "I have given Genet to Alemu. I want you to release her." So not long after I had thought the issue was settled, Regat asked me, "Has God said anything to you today?"

I said, "Yes. He said to love your enemies and pray for their salvation."

"I'm talking about something special or more personal."

"No, nothing specific. Why? Did you receive a message from the Lord for me?" At that time, Regat said, "No." She was afraid to tell me what the Lord had told her. My mom wasn't herself, either. She appeared to be wrestling with something. When the rest of us went to bed, she was still praying.

The next morning, Friday, was Christmas Day. My mom didn't want to talk with anyone. She clearly wasn't happy, and she looked as though she hadn't slept. We all went to church and returned home.

The conference was in session from Thursday through Sunday. Saturday, we all attended the church conference again. On Saturday afternoon I practiced with the choir, and my brother-in-law, Eyob, came in and called me out of the room. He said Alemu wanted to talk with me. I asked if Alemu was OK. Eyob had a big smile on his face. I asked him why he was smiling, but he didn't respond.

I went to see Alemu at the church office, and he was on his knees praying. I went in and knelt down and began to pray, as I had no clue why I was there. When Alemu finished praying, we stood up, and he said, "Thank you for coming."

Alemu started to look for a verse in his Bible and read from 2 Kings 10:15-17, "He greeted him and said to him, 'Is your heart right as my heart is toward your heart?' And Jehonadab answered, 'It is.' Jehu said, 'If it is, give me your hand.' So, he gave him his hand, and he took him up to him into the chariot. Then he said, 'Come with me, and see my zeal for the Lord.'"

Alemu stopped reading and said, "You know the call on my life. If you think you have the calling, I am asking you to come and let us serve the Lord together. If you don't think this is your calling, and you don't want to be with me, it is OK. I don't want you to feel obligated to give an answer that isn't right for you. And I don't want you to say anything about this to anyone. I would like you to pray about it, and let me know."

I was shocked, in fact stunned, but I said I would pray about it and thanked him. I left the office and couldn't stop crying. I felt I wasn't good enough or spiritual enough to be his wife and especially a minister's wife. I was afraid and confused as to what was going on. I told the Lord that it couldn't be from Him, because He knew I wasn't good enough to be a minister's wife.

On Sunday evening, the last day of the conference, a pastor friend told me that two months earlier he had a vision. In the vision, he said, "I saw you and Alemu holding hands dressed like a bride and groom walking together." He said to me, "I just want you to know that I don't know what it means, but God told me to pray about it and you should do what He tells you to do." I said, "Okay." It was a confirmation, but at the time, I didn't understand it.

Monday, I decided to fast and pray. I asked the Lord what was happening. I had four issues to bring before God as I prayed:

1. Lord, you know I can't marry Alemu, because he's not from my ethnic background. My parents won't let me, and

You know I prayed that I wouldn't be in a position where I would have to choose between You and my parents.

2. Lord, you know that my parents won't accept him.

3. Lord, you know that I'm not good enough to be Alemu's wife.

4. Lord, is this from the enemy who wants to destroy your servants, or is this from you?

As I mentioned previously, Alemu had been engaged, but his engagement was broken because of the girl's father. He didn't approve of Alemu's ethnic background. After Alemu broke the engagement and was flying back to the U.S. from Africa, he started praying on the airplane. He was praying about marrying, and decided not to pray about it anymore. He decided to serve the Lord alone as God's grace would enable him, but no more praying about marriage! While he was thinking about this, the Lord told him to forgive the girl's father and to bless him. Alemu did this, and immediately the Lord brought me to his mind. He started praying for me.

That isn't to say that Alemu understood why he was praying for me. He thought, "Why am I thinking about Genet? I don't know her that well. I don't know anything about her life. One thing I know is that she's an Eritrean, the same ethnic group as my former fiancée."

"Why am I praying for her? Lord, I don't want to get married at all, especially to an Eritrean. I don't want to deal with the hate that's between my people and those people. Besides, I don't know her."

The Lord kept telling him to keep praying, and then He told Alemu He had given me to him to be his wife.

Alemu struggled with that impression. He continued in prayer: "Lord, there's no way that I'm going to deal with this conflict again. I don't know her. I don't want to go through the same thing again."

Alemu kept arguing with the Lord and refused to pray about marrying. This happened in November 1986.

Just one month later, he was speaking at the church conference we've been talking about. The night before Christmas Eve, the Lord woke Alemu up at 2 a.m., the same time the Lord had been waking him up to pray about his earlier planned marriage, and the Lord told Alemu to ask me to marry him. Then Alemu said to the Lord, "I will ask her, but only under the following conditions.

1. You will be the elder to go ask her parents for her hand, because I won't send anyone.

2. You will deal with her parent's prejudice, so I won't have to.

3. Everyone will say this marriage must be from God.

4. Your Name will be glorified."

Alemu preached that Christmas Eve, on a Thursday. On Saturday, when reading the passage from 2 Kings to me, Alemu asked me to marry him.

My mother didn't want Alemu as a son-in-law, but the Lord kept convicting her of the hatred in her heart that kept her from accepting him. The same Saturday, December 26, 1986, the Lord said to my mother, "Take Alemu as your firstborn son, and I will bless you. He is pure in my sight. I have chosen Genet for him. I want you to accept him as your own firstborn son." When she heard this same voice again, the fear of the Lord came upon her. She prayed, "Lord, I fear you and I want to obey, but you have to heal my heart and change it, so that I can see him as your servant and accept him as my son." The Lord healed her heart and changed it.

The next morning, Sunday, when we got to church, she asked Alemu for forgiveness. They had never met, and he didn't know why she was apologizing. He said, "You haven't done anything against me. There is nothing to forgive." She insisted that he forgive her, so he said, "OK. I forgive you."

She hugged him and told him that she loved him. At this time, Alemu was thinking that I must have told her about his proposal. He imagined that my revealing his proposal to Mom was what triggered her request for forgiveness. He said to Mom, "I don't know what's going on, but I know the Lord is in charge." But at this point I hadn't told my mom anything. She knew only what the Lord had told her.

When the conference was over, everyone else returned home. Alemu changed his airline ticket and stayed to talk with my mother and me. On Monday he came to my sister Regat's home, where we were staying, but only my mother was at the house. When she opened the door and saw it was Alemu, she told him she knew why he came and invited him in. She told him what the Lord had told her, the entire story, that she approved of the marriage, and that she would accept

Alemu as her firstborn. Alemu told his story, that he had already asked me to be his wife, and that he was waiting for my response.

My mother told him that I was probably waiting and praying, because her children knew how she felt about the ethnic issues. Then she said, "I know Genet will obey God, no matter what." Alemu and my mom set the wedding date for July 18, 1987. They praised the Lord and spent a wonderful day together.

Later I returned to the house. When I walked in and saw them together, I started wondering if mother had said anything rude to Alemu. Before I finished the thought, my mother said to me, "Honey, it is OK with me and your father that you marry Alemu."

I almost passed out! I couldn't believe what I heard! I asked my mother if she knew where Alemu was from. She said, *yes,* she knew. She said she knew he was sent from the Lord, so it was OK. I was in awe! I said, "OK. I'm glad everybody heard from the Lord, but I need to hear from Him, too." Actually I had just heard the Lord, but it was overwhelming to believe what my mother had just said!

After a few days, I knew this was God's plan, and I was willing to obey. However, I felt I wasn't good enough to be Alemu's wife. I kept seeing Alemu behind the pulpit as I thought of him, so I believed it was wrong for me to think that he could be my husband.

I asked the Lord to let me see him as an ordinary man, so I could say *yes* to the proposal. The Lord changed my perception, and I told Alemu I would marry him.

No Specific Formula for Finding a Marriage Partner

On July 18, 1987, we were married. I can't tell the story any better than Genet does. There is no specific formula for knowing the will of God regarding a marriage partner, or anything important in your life. The purpose of telling you our story is to show how God brings His will into being for those who are sincere about starting right and running straight.

God brought us into a wonderful relationship that looked impossible from our backgrounds. Yet the right relationships in life are so important to God that He is ready to provide them to anyone who will allow Him the opportunity.

Therefore, in the process of marriage, the most important points include:

1. **The Starting Point.**

   This is knowing the will of God and accepting a person unconditionally. "The man said, 'This is now bone of my bones and flesh of my flesh; she shall be called a woman,' for she was taken out of man" (Genesis 2:23).

2. **Commitment to the Journey**

   Marriage is a lifelong journey to be sustained through unity and support. "For this reason, a man will leave his father and mother and be united to his wife, and they will become one flesh" (Genesis 2:24).

3. **Focusing on Prophetic Destiny.**

   God has a specific purpose for every family. Finding out and aiming for that goal gives a couple clearer direction and fulfillment. Knowing God's destiny enhances a couple's companionship, and the honesty God intends for every marriage. "The man and his wife were both naked and they felt no shame" (Genesis 2:25).

God is more than willing to reveal His will to us within the context of our circumstances, if we let him. Again, we are living proof. So, how is your covenant relationship?

CHAPTER 10

LIVING IN PROPHETIC DESTINY

I will make you into a great nation and I will bless
you; I will make your name great, and you will be a
blessing.

Genesis 12:2

I was blessed with a wonderful wife and very effective ministries. I was
working fulltime for CI, pastoring an Ethiopian church in Denver,
leading EESA, and founded Gospel of Glory ministry. Gospel of
Glory was birthed in 1991 after a visit to Ethiopia so I could do
research for a mission organization about the relief impact in an
underground church in Ethiopia during communism. The mission
organization, SIM, asked me and another missionary who lived and
worked in Ethiopia for many years to do this research. On our arrival
in Ethiopia, they rented a helicopter to travel to every corner of the
country. We did that in about two weeks. For this research, at every
place we visited, we met with church leaders who had been imprisoned

at the height of the persecution in different parts of Ethiopia. As I looked at these people, having neither training nor material resources, and their struggles, the Lord started showing about the challenges churches will face in Ethiopia because the lack of training.

During the last interview with six leaders, who had been in prison for five years, one of them said, "Today the Lord has answered our five years of prayer." When we asked what he meant, he told us about a prayer journey they had been on for five years. When they were in prison, they didn't have access to a Bible or any kind of spiritual books as it was forbidden by the government to do so. They survived by sharing a page from a Bible in a restroom with each other.

At that time, they decided to pray for the Lord to raise someone who would write spiritual books that are biblically sound and culturally relevant to help underground churches in Ethiopia. One of the men said, as he was looking into my eyes, with a great smile on his face, "Today, the Lord brought you here so that I would know my prayer has been answered." I said him, "What do you mean?" He replied, "Young man, you are the one God has prepared to write spiritual books to equip the Body of Christ in Ethiopia." I quickly replied, "No sir. I am not a writer." The only thing I had written at that time was a small book in Amharic, *Christ in The Tabernacle,* and my doctoral dissertation. He didn't respond. He just smiled back.

I came back and shared the burden I sensed with Genet. After we sought the Lord in prayer, we decided to use our savings and write one book that we felt would be helpful to the underground church. The title in English was *Spiritual Leadership.* After we published the book, we started smuggling them in through friends and missionaries. I thought that was it, but the demand for more books increased beyond our capacity and resources. We started praying and seeking the Lord again and the advice of people we trusted, including the person who had hired me. After I heard from many of my friends, I went to Mr. Erickson, President of CI. When I told him what was going on, he said, "Alemu, don't confuse your calling with an employment. Organizations like CI hire, but a true calling is only from God. I believe the Lord is calling you to respond to the needs of the underground church."

That day Genet and I stopped fighting the call of God. We embraced the call **to equip Christian leaders and empower the Body of Christ to serve God's purpose and impact their generation.**

The Lord had spoken about such an assignment specifically in 1985, the year I graduated from with my Ph.D. In August of 1985, I was one of the speakers at the EESA annual conference in Chicago. After I finished speaking during one of the general sessions before I closed in prayer, a minister who the Lord used mightily as a revivalist during the socialism in Ethiopia, raised his hand, "I have a short word from the Lord." I asked him to come forward and release the word. He started by saying, "I usually don't give personal prophecy publicly; I share with individuals in private. But today the Lord instructed me to speak in public. A very short prophecy I received form the Lord for you. I saw the Lord putting on you a garment of many colors, like Joseph. The Lord is confirming your calling to the nations."

After we decided to establish a nonprofit Christian organization, we started praying for the ministry name and focus. That is when the Lord gave us the name **Gospel of Glory**. We incorporated Gospel of Glory in 1991 as a nonprofit Christian organization with the objective of declaring His glory among the nations by moving leaders from ordinary ministry activates to extraordinary relationship with God. We incorporated with the following:

1. **Mission**

   To empower the Body of Christ and equip Christian leaders to serve God's purpose and impact their generations (Acts 13:36).

2. **Vision**

   To find, raise and equip transformational leaders of all ages who have the calling, gifting, and character to make a significant impact on society for the Kingdom of God in strategic regions of the world.

3. **Core Value**

   It's about His Gospel, and we will not mix it. It's about His glory, and we will not touch it.

4. **Core Strategies**

   To find, raise, mentor, equip and train leaders and mobilize the Body of Christ for the fullness of His glory!

   • **Revitalizing Vision**

   Revitalizing leaders' visions in strategic regions of the world for sustainable transformation of the community at large. We do this by providing biblically sound, culturally relevant books to unite leaders who were trapped in past experiences like Lazarus. "Take off the grave clothes and let him go" (John 11:44).

- **Mentoring**

  Preparing effective change agents by mentoring young leaders to expand and enhance transformational leaders' visions for transforming leadership. That would be similar to personal transformation and true identity by taking off Saul's arms and walk in their own anointing and calling, like David.

- **Empowering**

  Empowering the Body of Christ to declare and demonstrate the power of the Gospel of Jesus Christ. Establishing a center for equipping, modeling and sending out leaders with new vision and value to make a difference in their generation.

- **Spiritual Accountability Network**

  Mentoring emerging young people to start on biblical foundations and to finish well including the correction of wrong practices, making history by establishing a standard of excellence and shaping the future.

After that time, my burden grew into our present fulltime ministry through Gospel of Glory. Since the inception of Gospel of Glory in 1991, I had served CI in program development as I continued ministering to leaders in and around the Ethiopian population ministering to leaders around the world. Today, the network has expanded into different countries in six continents through a variety of organizations. I was fully devoted to Christian leadership development and building the capacity in local churches to fulfill the Great Commission. Over the years, my biggest burden has been for leaders to know their calling, have a clear vision, a caring and loving heart, a sound mind, to know their gifts and use them with a pure motive and attitude. That means equipping them with materials like books, CDs, DVDs, broadcasts and teaching that will truly encourage them to impact but not to necessarily impress. Since 1991, we have published and provided more than 40 books and materials in Amharic, English, Spanish, Thai and Indonesian.

My calling is really very simple, and straightforward. I want to do everything in my power to assist the local church to fulfill its mission, and especially to encourage those Christians in leadership. Encouraging leaders in the church, business and government to know their identity and walk with the Lord in an extraordinary relationship. Together, we must understand our spiritual authority and keep our anointing.0-

Since 1991 until the year 2000, I was leading this ministry and working for CI fulltime. In 2000, Genet and I took a step of faith and focused on Gospel of Glory ministries fulltime in order to carry out our calling.

The same year we established Gospel of Glory ministries to fulfill our biblical mandate, the Lord blessed us with a beautiful daughter, Keah Alemu Beeftu. Keah was born February 15, 1991.

Keah means *my own*. When we take a step of faith to obey, He releases special blessings into our lives. In 1993, the Lord added His blessings by giving us Ammanuel Alemu Beeftu. The birth of Ammanuel (Emmanuel in English) put a stamp of assurance on the presence of God with us. As Genet became busy with our two children, I continued traveling to the nations. All along we have witnessed the fulfillment of the promises of Abraham. The proper path to prosperity is obedience to the will and the purpose of God.

> I will make you into a great nation and I will bless you;
> I will make your name great, and you will be a blessing.
>
> Genesis 12:2

After the curse of Earth because of Adam's sin, the second worst sign of poverty took place when the Lord destroyed all creation with the Great Flood. During Noah's time when the Lord saw the evilness of human hearts, He saved Noah and his family and destroyed all living things. After the Great Flood, the Lord made a covenant of blessings with Noah, and afterward the Lord established a lasting covenant of blessings with Abraham. The core of this covenant was to restore, through redemptive work, the blessings of creation by paying the price for the covenant. Since the worst form of poverty is separation from God, He chose Abraham. He called Abraham as a point of contact to bring back the blessings through His son all the blessings intended at the beginning. The covenant was to remove the curse of sin and bring back blessings of creation and prosperity.

Christ redeemed us from the curse of the law by becoming a curse for us, for it is written: "Cursed is everyone who is hung on a tree. He redeemed us in order that the blessing given to Abraham might come to the Gentiles through Christ Jesus, so that by faith we might receive the promise of the Spirit."

Galatians 3:13-14

These verses are the fulfillment of God's covenant with Abraham when he received his calling that he would be a blessing to all humanity (Genesis 12:1-3). This is called covenantal blessings. Both in creation and in covenant, God's purpose has been, from the beginning, to bless human beings and make them blessings for all creation. The covenantal blessings started with the call of God, which I refer to in this book, *Breakout for Breakthrough: Journey for Prophetic Destiny*. In other words, like in Genesis, God was the initiator of covenantal blessings. In creation, He created Adam to manage the blessings. In covenant, He set apart Abraham and made him the father of many nations to release blessings to the world. Since this was a covenant, it required Abraham's response. Abraham accepted the call for covenantal blessings by faith. In order to enter into the blessings God prepared for humanity, Abraham had to leave his country by faith for a new country of covenant and inheritance. His people for new generations to come could not be counted, "I will make your offspring like the dust of the earth, so that if anyone could count the dust, then your offspring could be counted." His country would become a father of many nations and a friend of God. His father's household would be a new city that would come from God, the promise giver. Without details for the future, he went on a journey of his prophetic destiny.

Covenant blessing or prosperity started with a nation or generation. In God's economy, people or a generation is the greatest blessing. From the beginning, God's desire is to have a family. Because of sin, the family relationship was broken. God called Abraham to raise a nation for Himself in order to establish the family relationship through covenant with Abraham, so that we can became sons and daughters to become a blessing by fulfilling our calling. That was the reason why Genet and I said *yes* to the call of God to establish Gospel of Glory to become a blessing to nations as we declare His glory.

Since its inception, Gospel of Glory has been the source of blessings to the Body of Christ and Christian leaders around the world. Every year thousands are coming into the Kingdom of light through this ministry, in addition to equipping and mobilizing Kingdom workers and change agents.

That is what the Lord has been affirming through his prophets as well. Here is one example. "Your calling will never be an easy one, Alemu and Genet, because you will never be allowed to focus just on this house, and you know that. You will always be required to think Kingdom first; big picture; nations. You just keep your eyes on the vision, and don't worry about the provision."

Dutch Sheets

CHAPTER 11

BLESSINGS OF OBEDIENCE FOR PROPHETIC
DESTINY

The King will say to those on his right, "Come, you
who are blessed by my Father; take your inheritance,
the Kingdom prepared for you since the creation of the
world.'

Matthew 25:34

Welcome to Prosper to Prosper

My daughter was born the same year we started the ministry of Gospel
of Glory, 1991. She graduated from high school, May 2008. The
graduation ceremony was held at the U.S. Air Force Academy in
Colorado Springs. We went about two hours early to get a good seat
to take pictures. More than that, I was excited about my daughter
completing high school. In my family, I am the only person who has
earned a college degree. Now my daughter is the only girl who has
attended school. It was an amazing day for me.

While we were waiting, I received a telephone call from a very good friend. I stepped outside to talk since I had time before the graduation ceremony started. He shared with me what he felt the Lord had said about Gospel of Glory's transition that morning. After hanging up the phone, I started walking and praying, since we had at least more than an hour before the graduation ceremony.

During that time, the Lord started speaking to me about Gospel of Glory's transition. I heard the Lord whispering into my spirit saying that Gospel of Glory is also going to be graduated just like your daughter and move away for a greater purpose. After graduation, I shared with my wife what I heard about relocation of the ministry from Colorado Springs to another city. Naturally, I thought the Lord would like us to move to Denver to be closer to the international airport because of my travel schedule. Of course, that would make it very convenient.

However, that was not what the Lord had in mind. In the meantime, other voices started coming about Dallas. Our close friend and Gospel of Glory's board member told us that she was considering moving to Dallas area. At this point, we decided to start praying very seriously with other intercessors. While this was going on, Apostle Greg Hood came from Hawaii with his wife for a doctor appointment and stayed with us. That evening as we were praying for his wife Joan's health, Greg got up and started looking for a piece of paper and pencil. At the end of our prayer time he gave it to me a paper with these writing on it:

Denver: Where a familiar spirit lives.

Washington D.C.: Where the future seed will be plated.

Dallas: Where like-minded walk together to do Kingdom work.

After I read that message, I knew the Lord was serious about moving Gospel of Glory's headquarters from Colorado Springs to the Dallas area. Then I knew, Denver would be out of the equation. The time and season for the Washington D.C. assignment was not yet. The same week I was asked to speak at Wagner Leadership Institute about "Transition for transformation. new season, new promises and new focus."

After that workshop, we decided to invite some intercessors and other powerful leaders to meet with us in Denton, Texas to help us discern if what we were hearing is from the Lord. The next day before our meeting with the prayer team, we went out to drive around to get some feel for the greater Dallas area. We drove from Denton on Highway 380 East until we saw a sign, "Welcome to Prosper to Prosper." Yes, of course, we turned into the town of Prosper and drove down Colman Street to see Prosper High School. Since our son was a senior in high school, one of our concerns was his high school. The high school looked like college building, and it looked new. We liked the name of the town and the high school. It was a great start for the first day.

That evening we went to have dinner with our great friends, Cindy and Mike Jacobs. After dinner, Cindy asked us if we made a decision about a city where we would like to settle. She tried to encourage us to consider Red Oak, south of Dallas. I told her that we hadn't made any decision since we are still seeking the will of God and confirmation about our move. We told her that although we hadn't made a decision, we went to the town of Prosper, and we were very impressed with the town billboard, **"Welcome to Prosper to Prosper."** She commented, "Where is that?" After we described the location, Cindy sensed the following in her spirit and spoke it.

> "Prosper, prosper, prosper! Of course! It's Prosper. And then when you said God is going to take them to a place where they would prosper, the anointing just hit me. Prosper! That's why I asked you because that just hit me so hard; if you felt anything about Prosper.
>
> "And the Lord would say there is prosperity in Prosper; there is prosperity in Prosper! And I would have you at the beginning; the beginning of the prosperity."

That was the first conformation we received. The next day on November 24, 2009 at 11 a.m. in Denton at Glory of Zion we met at the Momentum Conference room with 12 intercessors for prayer to hear the Lord. After an hour of prayer time, although we planned for three hours, everybody said that this is from the Lord. At that point, we fully embraced the call of the Lord to move to the greater Dallas area in obedience to the will of God.

Welcome to Prosper

Proper path to prosperity is to be in the center of the will of God. That includes geographical location to enjoy his blessings. When Adam sinned, God's question was not "What did you?" or "Why did you disobey?" but it was "Where are you?" Being in the right place positions us for the blessings of God in the will of God. That is why we pray, "Let your kingdom come and Your will be done." Yes, the biblical sign, for every child of God, is "Welcome to the Kingdom of blessings." The Lord who welcomes us into the Kingdom of light will say to us one of these days,

> "The King will say to those on his right, "Come, you who are blessed by my Father; take your inheritance, the kingdom prepared for you since the creation of the world."

> Matthew 25:34

The proper path to prosperity is to become as a child by faith and accept His plan of blessings. "I know the plans I have for you," declares the LORD, "Plans to prosper you and not to harm you, plans to give you hope and a future" (Jeremiah 29:11). For this reason, the core of our calling is to receive His blessings and prosper in His presence.

> Know that to this you have been called, that you may yourselves inherit a blessing [from God—that you

may obtain a blessing as heirs, bringing welfare and happiness and protection].

1 Peter 3:9 AMP

It is important to understand some of the principles that reveal His plans. Apostle John expressed this by saying, "Beloved, I pray that you may prosper in all things and be in health, just as your soul prospers" (3 John 2). God revealed His heart's desire to bless and prosper His children through:

- Creation
- Covenant
- Declarations
- Kingdom Principles
- Second Coming Promise

The proper path to prosper is to live according to the original design at creation, to be grounded on the covenant foundation, hear and walk in the powerful revelation of the Word of God by the Holy Spirit, understand and practice Kingdom principles, and walk in clearer vision of the promised blessing that is yet to be revealed.

But we must overcome some of challenges that come to stop us from having breakthrough. For me and my family, one of the greatest blessings was moving to Texas after almost 22 years in order to do His will. By moving, we gave up everything to start all over again in obedience. Even though we had lived in Colorado Springs most of our married life, we embraced the call to Texas. However, we faced several huge challenges. The first challenge was, humanly speaking, the timing was wrong. The housing market had a huge downturn not only in our area but throughout the U.S. Putting the house on the market was extremely bad timing. As the result, to obey God we lost $100,000 on the sale of our house! Because of the house market situation, ministry support suddenly dropped. It felt as if somebody turned off a water pipe. All this put the ministry for the first time in the red, by $40,000. I kept traveling for ministry because of the commitment we made. Suddenly, we realized our finances were on "life support." We felt our dreams were approaching death, and immediately. But this made it so clear, we would definitely move to Texas. Obedience to our prophetic destiny is costly and scary! While we were struggling, the Lord sent Pastor Samuel Brassfield to speak "life" into our situation. He built our faith with just a few words,

"Sell what you can sell! What you buy is on me."

Genet and I came off life support. Our dreams were coming to life again. After taking the initiative to move, the Lord gave us so much more! It wasn't always easy, but we lived on our dreams and the word of the Lord that Pastor Samuel Brassfield had spoken.

The Lord Told Me to Meet Your Personal Need

The Lord made everything new for us just as he spoke through Cindy Jacobs: a home for us without consistent income, new Christian private school for our son, new office without rent for Gospel of Glory, etc. As we settled into our new place, we started rebuilding the ministry as our daughter's graduation approached faster than we would have liked. The concern was that once she graduated, we are obligated to start paying the school loan. School loans for both our children became our reach. But we didn't know what to do, except trust the Lord walk by faith. Before we left Colorado. the Lord promised us that He would take care of our children. While we were praying for these concerns, I went overseas on a ministry trip. At the end of that ministry time, a Christian brother asked if we could meet for lunch before I would fly back home. We went out for lunch and shared and prayed together, and I also prayed for the new business initiative he was thinking about starting. Finally, we stopped to eat lunch. During the time, he asked me a question that surprised me. He said, "What is your personal need?" I responded by telling him all the ministry needs we have. He said that the Lord told him specifically to meet the personal needs and concerns I have. I said, "Brother, as you know, we live by faith, so I really don't know what to say." We finished our lunch and went for coffee. While we were drinking our coffee, he started sharing with me prayer requests for his children. After I promised to pray for his family, I shared with him about my children and our concern for their school loan payments that would start soon. As soon as I finished my statement, he said "That is the personal need the Lord would like me to help you with." I was speechless! I didn't know what to say. Instead of saying thank you so much, I responded by saying "College tuition is very expensive in the USA, and I have two children in college." He said, "Don't worry just send me original receipts from the loan offices, and I will take care of it." I was astonished. I inquired, "You are sure?" He answered, "Yes, I am sure."

He dropped me off at the hotel and went home. I called Genet and told her what had happened. She was shocked and speechless as well. She kept asking me by saying, "Are you sure? Is that what he said?"

I came home and scanned all the loan statements. In the email, I restated again, because of the amount, to feel free to help with whatever amount without feeling obligated. He sent me an email the same week stating that checks had been sent to loan offices for the total amount of $84,000. He also said, "Send us every semester the original billing statement until they have completed their undergraduate studies." Subsequently, both of our children graduated with their BA degrees without any debt.

After the children's school tuition was paid, we faced a transportation challenge. I gave my old car to my son since I was not able buy him another car. We tried with one car, but because of the ministry's demands, it became impossible. We started praying and looking online for a used dependable car. I couldn't find anything that we could afford. One morning during my devotion as I was praying for a car, I heard the voice of the Holy Spirit, "I have prepared a table before you, but you are focusing on crumbs on the floor." I rose up from my prayer and asked, "Lord, is that your voice? I believe it is. Please lead me and show me what to do to enjoy what you have prepared for me." I felt to look for a website of an expensive car deal. I saw a commercial on the home page, a one-day special sale. It was the car I liked the first time I saw it. Since I didn't know the price, I decided to be quiet until I went to see it. The car's first owner of had a very minor accident, and he traded in for a new car. Because of the accident, the dealer didn't want to certify the sale. Since it was expensive, the dealership decided to get rid of it in a day. I went and purchased the car for an unbelievably low price. I am still driving it. Yes, He the is protector and provider on our prophetic destiny.

The blessings of obedience to fulfill prophetic destiny are real!

CHAPTER 12

MANAGING BLESSINGS OF PROPHETIC DESTINY

He was faithful to the one who appointed him, just as Moses was faithful in all God's house.

Hebrews 3:2

The only way we can fulfill our prophetic destiny is through faith and faithfulness to our calling. Faith is the foundation as children of God. From the time I was saved, I placed my trust in the Word of God. If I read it, the Word of God for me is the promise. From the beginning, I didn't have anything, but the promises of God. When I didn't know where to go or what to do, I stood on the Word of God. Since I accepted the Lord, the enemy always is too late. I was born late, started school late, I married late, I had children late, etc., and God redeemed it for His plan and purpose. You get the picture. I have verses that have been the foundation of my faith since faith isn't personal assumptions or desires. For my faith, I hear clearly the promises of God and stand firm on His words. One those verses is,

> He will be the sure foundation for your times, a rich
> store of salvation and wisdom and knowledge; the fear
> of the LORD is the key to this treasure.

Isaiah 33:6

To build our faith on the Word of the Lord, we should walk in the true fear and reverence of God.

I am on my journey because of my faith in the One who has called me and set me apart for His glory. But on this journey for our prophetic destiny, I have a travel insurance with Policy No. 1TH5-24. It reads this way, "The one who calls you is faithful, and he will do it" (1 Thessalonians 5:24). I haven't left the house without it since I started this journey. It works in every circumstance.

Yes, faith is the foundation for my journey and destiny. But trust has been the source of my peace and confidence on this journey. For me, trust is all about an ongoing relationship with the Lord. Because of my trust in Him, I want to be faithful to Him in every way. I honor Him through my trust! I please God by faith! I serve His will by being faithful. God measures faithfulness in fulfilling our prophetic destiny. The conclusion of both Jesus' and Moses' ministries was faithfulness as it is written,

> He was faithful to the one who appointed him, just as
> Moses was faithful in all God's house.

Hebrews 3:2

One of the greatest things on the journey of our destiny is to manage faithfully spiritual, material, and human resources. The original plan and purpose of God in creation is to prosper those who He created after His own likeness to reflect His glorious image (2 Corinthians 3:18), and manage His resources. God created and restored Earth for five days before He created mankind. Everything He created for five days was given to human beings with a command to increase, multiply and fill Earth and manage it. "The Lord God took the man and put him in the Garden of Eden to tend and guard and keep it" (Genesis 2:15). The fact is that God placed mankind in a garden where we are created to prosper.

God created everything not just to meet daily needs for mankind, but for enjoyment. "Out of the ground the Lord God made to grow every tree that is pleasant to the sight or to be desired—good (suitable, pleasant) for food" (Genesis 2:9 AMP). Our God is a good and generous God. He enjoys the joy of His children. That is why He didn't create and place mankind on Earth that was formless, empty and covered with darkness. But He restored Earth and removed the darkness first before He gave it to Adam to manage. The five days of creation show how much God wanted man to enjoy the blessings. The journey of our prophetic destiny is to enter into that plan and dwell in it. The greatest prosperity is to enjoy the gift of God and manage it for His glory and honor. There is no greater gift.

Furthermore, God blessed Adam and Eve to be fruitful. It is not limited to what was created at that time, but God gave us the power to multiply and have authority over everything. King David put it this way, "You made him ruler over the works of your hands; you put everything under his feet" (Psalm 8:6). Mankind is given power to prosper as well as authority to rule Earth and creation for the glory of God. God involved Adam in the creation process by asking him to name the animals. "He brought them to the man to see what he would name them; and whatever the man called each living creature, that was its name" (Genesis 2:19). Naming all creation and multiplying the garden to fill all Earth with it were true signs of property and wealth. That was given to mankind at creation. In other words, poverty was not part of the creation plan.

God also gave mankind the keys to prosper and stay blessed. One of the keys that He gave was to honor Him with their blessings, the resources of Earth. That is making the Creator first by declaring His lordship through daily relationship and the firstfruits offering. The two sons of Adam clearly understood this. However, Cain decided to worship the Lord not the way God wanted, but the way Cain, himself, wanted. Because of his disobedience sin, he took charge over his life, and he became the first poorest person in human history by killing his brother. Relational poverty with God and family members is the worst forms of poverty. He was the first person to kill one third of the human race, because he didn't want to worship the Lord according to the revealed will of God.

The beginning and the end of true prosperity is to make the Creator the Redeemer and Sustainer of everything first by declaring His ownership. We do this by our firstfruits offerings and our tithe. That is part of managing the resources. We make Him the first by honoring Him with our firstfruits. "Honor the LORD with your wealth, with the firstfruits of all your crops; then your barns will be filled to overflowing, and your vats will brim over with new wine" (Proverbs 3:9-10).

That was what Noah did after the Great Flood. This particular flood was the result of rebelling against God. Only one person found favor in God's eyes, because He walked in righteousness. The world became poor in relationship with God because of sin. God sent the Great Flood to destroy all creation except Noah and family. Noah prospered in the middle of a sinful generation, who rejected God, because of his fear and reverence for the Lord. He prospered in the middle of a changing situation while the rest of humanity was destroyed by flooding. Noah was faithful to God, and God was faithful in saving him and his family. That is a true prosperity.

Before he started enjoying the blessings of God, when he came out of the ark, he made a sacrifice to the Lord. In other words, he started with God. He concluded 120 years of obedience by building altar and presenting a holy sacrifice of worship. No wonder, God smelled the pleasing aroma of his firstfruits sacrifice and made the following declaration to prosper him and his generation.

- Promised not to curse Earth and destroy creation with a flood again. In other words, extended His mercy to humanity in spite of the inclination of human hearts because of the Noah's sacrifice.

- Promised to change seasons for lasting blessings. "As long as the earth endures, seedtime and harvest, cold and heat, summer and winter, day and night will never cease" (Genesis 8:22).

- Promised to bless Noah and His children (Genesis 9:1).

- He gave them authority over creation (Genesis 9:1).

- He established lasting covenant with Noah and His descendants (Genesis 9:9).

- He gave Noah a sign of lasting covenant, a rainbow. That rainbow is still with us and for us because of Noah's obedience in making the Lord first. A true sign of prosperity is having something we can pass to the next generation.

Mankind is created in His image, which is the greatest prosperity and blessing, to manage His resources by making Him first in everything. Prosperity starts with knowing who we are, our true identity in God. A person who doesn't know their identity in God can't manage God's blessings and resources. That is why the worst form of poverty is identity crisis. Usually, people kill themselves and abuse and kill others not because of lack of resources but because of an identity crisis. That is why true blessings don't start with earthly resources, but with spiritual blessings. "Praise be to the God and Father of our Lord Jesus Christ, who has blessed us in the heavenly realms with every spiritual blessing in Christ" (Ephesians 1:3). Spiritual blessings in Christ Jesus restores our true identity so that we can honor God with our resources and become a blessing to others.

The Responsibility of Handling Creation Prosperity

The blessings of God come with possibilities. We enjoy the creation blessings by:

1. **Recognizing God as the Creator and honor Him in everything.**

   "The earth is the LORD'S, and everything in it, the world, and all who live in it" (Psalm 24:1). Mankind has been given the responsibility of stewardship, not ownership. God is the Owner who ought to be honored by everything we are given to manage. God-honoring resources management requires faithfulness and trust worthiness. The parable of the talents in Matthew 25:14-17 is the best example of this. The owner gave five talents of money, to another two and another one. At the end, he rewarded the first two according to their faithfulness in multiplying what they were given. However, the one who received one talent was punished not because of the amount, but because of laziness. Laziness is a sign of carelessness and unfaithfulness.

2. **Using resources for the Glory of God.**

   God created Earth for His glory and gave to Adam to rule and manage for the glory of the Creator. The responsibility was to do everything for the glory of God in the spirit of worship. Paul recorded this for the New Testament believers, "Whether you eat or drink or whatever you do, do it all for the glory of God" (1 Corinthians 10:31).

3. **Using resources to declare His Lordship.**

   God prospers us so that we can manage the prosperity to make Him first. The concept of managing prosperity is to use our resources to worship Him as the Creator and King of the Universe. Adam started that way by using the garden as a place of fellowship and worship. "When the man and his wife heard the sound of the LORD God as he was walking in the garden in the cool of the day" (Genesis 3:8). Honoring the Lord with our best is called the firstfruits. "Honor the LORD with your wealth, with the firstfruits of all your crops; then your barns will be filled to overflowing, and your vats will brim over with new wine" (Proverbs 3:9-10). Through firstfruits giving, we declare who He is in our lives, our total dependence upon Him and our faith and trust in Him.

4. **Living a life of obedience.**

   The best of way of keeping and multiplying the prosperity God has given us is by obeying His voice. That means do with the resources whatever He asks us to do. When He says *give,* we give; when He says *multiply*, we invest in Kingdom work through our firstfruits, tithing, love gifts and helping the poor.

5. **Protect God's resources.**

   After the Lord gave mankind dominion to rule Earth and bless him to be fruitful; He placed him in the garden. "The LORD God took the man and put him in the Garden of

Eden to work it and take care of it" (Genesis 2:15). We are given responsibilities of protecting and multiplying the resources God entrusted to us by being in the right place and doing the right things. Adam was in the garden; the right place, but didn't do the right thing. By having the right attitude about the resources, God wants us to manage. Adam was asked to work it and care for it. Fruitfulness and multiplication are the result of this. It is very important to view prosperity as a management responsibility of God's resources in a total obedience daily to the reveled will of God.

6. **Be a channel of His blessings.**

Adam was blessed by God and given power and dominion on Earth to fill Earth with God's blessings. The responsibility is to become the channel of God's blessings to others; particularly, to the poor. Some of the root problems are selfishness, greediness, lack of trust and faith in God, lack of clear vision and purpose, etc. God's blessings are like living waters that have channels to flow through to bring hope, refreshment, life and fruitfulness (Ezekiel 47:6-12).

7. **Stay in your garden.**

Yes, Adam was given full dominion of Earth, but he was placed in the garden in order to be prosperous. He was exceedingly prosperous as long as he stayed, protected and cared for the Garden of Eden. One of the responsibilities in handling God's blessings is to stay in God's will. In the case of Adam, he was out of the Garden of Eden because he mishandled God's resources. The Lord assigned His angel to prevent Adam from coming back into the Garden of Eden. However, the second Adam, the Lord Jesus Christ, became the door and gave us access to the blessings of God through our relationship with Him. Because of our relationship with Him, mankind was given authority to manage not only material things but spiritual gifts as well. This mandate is an everlasting mandate.

From the beginning of my prophetic journey, I have taken managing the Lord's resources very seriously. Managing what God has given me is not about the quantity, but about being faithful with what He has given me. This is what I learned at the beginning of my Christian walk; out of hundred percent, ten percent is the Lord's. I made a commitment to manage that one dollar out of ten for the glory of God. That became the principle of my life in everything. On our journey Genet and I live by giving. Every time we have a major need, we ask each other what to give. Once I wrote a Bible study book about discipleship for churches without pastors. But we didn't have money to publish it and send to Ethiopian churches worldwide. While we prayed for provision, we went to attend a conference organized by our pastor. At the end of the conference, there was a special appeal for his ministry. We had $800 in our savings. We looked at each other. Usually, when that happens the Lord is speaking to us. I asked Genet how much. She says, "$800." I replied, "Okay!" We wrote a check. The following weekend we went to Washington DC to attend a Glory Fire conference. After the conference, I was asked to speak on Sunday afternoon at a local church.

However, that morning I felt the prompting of the Holy Spirit to go to another church and be ready to speak. I prepared a message and went to that church. I know that pastor, but I hadn't see him for a long time. We went and arrived before the pastor came in. When he saw me, his greeting was very warm and said, "I wish I had known that you were going to be here this morning, I could have asked you to speak." I responded that he should have no worries.

After the worship, the pastor greeted people before the offering. He called my name, greeted me and told the people he didn't know that I would be with them that morning. Then said, "If I had known, I would have asked him to speak." Pausing he said, "Even now if you have a message, and if you are willing…." Before the pastor finished his statement, the congregation started applauding. Since I had heard from the Lord, I spoke that morning. After I finished, the pastor said, "Please sow into Gospel of Glory a financial blessing as you leave." In five minutes people gave $8,000. Genet and I gave $800 the week before and received $8,000 to publish the book. This has been our experience all our lives.

The other aspect of managing faithfully God's resources, including working hard, is using what we have received. Working hard also means maximizing every opportunity to do the will of God and fulfill our calling. In my case, I didn't have options or choices and had to maximize every opportunity that came my way. It was the issue of survival. If I didn't take what was in my path and work with it as hard as possible, I would not have made it.

From the start, I pushed to attend school, and I put my best effort to stay in school. When I was given an opportunity to work for a missionary and stay in school, I pushed it so I could buy my Bible. Every time challenges intensified; I was determined even more to move forward. I remember in elementary school, most of the time my brother's son and I didn't have anything to eat. During lunch hour when students went for lunch, we would go to a river. After we prayed, we drank that water for our lunch. Sometimes that was all I had for a few days. Because of a sense of purpose, I was determined that the brown dirty river water would help us to survive. I considered that as my meal. That is maximizing what I have given by trusting the Lord for His grace.

In this regard, I always stand on the two promises of God.

He said to me, "My grace is sufficient for you, for my power is made perfect in weakness." Therefore, I will boast all the more gladly about my weaknesses, so that Christ's power may rest on me."

2 Corinthians 12:9

I personally believe that with a true call of God, the grace of God is always available. That grace brings the provision I need to complete the journey and fulfill the calling. The second passage is,

Well done, good and faithful servant! You have been faithful with a few things; I will put you in charge of many things. Come and share your master's happiness!

Matthew 25:23

A true sign of faithfulness is to honor the Lord by working wholeheartedly, and at the same time use what He has entrusted into my hands. The increase is the result of faithfulness with what we are given. As I obey, the Lord gives increase, and I harvest the fruits in the due time.

CHAPTER 13

PROPHETIC DESTINY AND HIS KINGDOM

They will make war against the Lamb, but the
Lamb will overcome them because he is Lord of
lords and King of kings—and with him will be his
called, chosen and faithful followers.

Revelation 17:14

Starting Right

As I mentioned in earlier chapters, an effective journey has three things
in common; starting point, identifiable process and achievable
destination. I learned early in my life; if in fact, my journey is to honor
and glorify the Lord, I should start in the right place. The right starting
place is true relationship with the Lord Jesus, who is *the Author and
Finisher of my faith, my good Shepherd, Savior, Emmanuel and Light*. It was
not because of knowledge or understanding I started with the Lord at
a young age. The Lord cleared the way for me to encounter Him when
I heard, "Who can abide with You, O God?" (Psalm 15). From the

mouth of a math teacher when I was in second grade! That day I started my journey on solid ground by giving my life to Christ. That was the true starting place. It marked a turning point in my life by breaking generational curses off my life. Breakout for breakthrough in seeking the Kingdom.

In this process, the most important thing for me has been obeying wholeheartedly to what was revealed to me. Until we have a true relationship with God through the forgiveness of sin, we haven't really started much of anything.

For me, the starting point was my relationship with the Lord and surrendering to His will. The divine invitation is, "Seek first the kingdom of God and His righteousness, and all these things shall be added to you" (Matthew 6:33). I started seeking the Kingdom to live under the authority of the King by doing His will. I received His righteousness by establishing my right standing with Him. I made my focus to understand the nature and manifestation of His kingdom.

After I started with the King, I made an effort to comprehend the basic characteristics of His kingdom. Understanding the King and the nature of His kingdom has enabled me to stay in His will. When I talk about Kingdom, in general, I'm referring to the King, His subjects, His territory or land and the law of the land. God is the Ruler and King of the Universe. Heavens are the place of His throne while Earth is His footstool. He gave Earth to mankind to rule and manage for His glory. At present, since darkness also has rulership, as a child of God, I should understand the nature of the Kingdom. That is why I believe the Kingdom of God starts with spiritual relationship. The Holy Spirit is the manager of the Kingdom of God. The Lord Jesus Christ is the King in the Kingdom, and God the Father is the Designer of the Kingdom. Hence, when I accepted the King of Glory, the Lord Jesus Christ as my Lord, I entered into His kingdom. His kingdom characteristics include the following:

- **Kingdom of rulership**

  "The LORD has established His throne in Heaven, and His kingdom rules over all" (Psalm 103:19; Daniel 5:21).

- **Kingdom of glory**

  "They will tell of the glory of your kingdom" (Psalm 145:11).

- **Kingdom of power or might**

  "Speak of your might" (Psalm 145:11).

- **Kingdom of majesty**

  "The glorious majesty of His kingdom" (Psalm 145:12).

- **Kingdom of all ages**

  "Your kingdom is an everlasting kingdom" (Psalm145:12; Daniel 4:3).

- **Kingdom for all generations**

  "Your dominion endures through all generations" (Psalm 145:13, Daniel 4:3).

- **Kingdom that endures**

  "His kingdom will not be destroyed" (Daniel 6:26).

- **Kingdom of governing**

  "His dominion will never end" (Daniel 6:26).

- **Kingdom life**

  "Jesus answered, 'I tell you the truth, no one can enter the kingdom of God unless he is born of water and the Spirit'" (John 3:5).

- **Kingdom of the Lordship of Christ**

  "They will make war against the Lamb, but the Lamb will overcome them because he is Lord of lords and King of kings—and with him will be his called, chosen and faithful followers" (Revelation 17:14).

- **Kingdom of forgiveness**

  "God exalted him to his own right hand as Prince and Savior that he might give repentance and forgiveness of sins to Israel" (Acts 5:31).

- **Kingdom of His will**

  "Your kingdom come, your will be done on earth as it is in heaven" (Matthew 6:10).

- **Kingdom power**

  "For the kingdom of God is not a matter of talk but of power" (1 Corinthians 4:20).

- **Kingdom of love**

  "By this all men will know that you are my disciples, if you love one another" (John 13:35).

- **Kingdom of unity**

  "My prayer is not for them alone. I pray also for those who will believe in me through their message, that all of them may be one" (John 17:20-21).

- **Kingdom of light**

  "The people living in darkness have seen a great light; on those living in the land of the shadow of death light has dawned" (Matthew 4:16).

- **Kingdom of peace**

  "Prince of Peace. Of the increase of his government and peace there will be no end" (Isaiah 9:6-7).

- **Kingdom of blessings**

  "Seek first his kingdom and his righteousness, and all these things will be given to you as well" (Matthew 6:33).

The restoration Jesus brought includes right relationship with Him that leads us into full Kingdom authority. Mankind was created for relationship and received dominion to rule Earth for the glory of God on the basis of relationship with God. That is what I entered into at the beginning of my journey.

Starting in the right place has given me on this journey clearer mission, vision, core values, direction, healthy and big dreams, passion to see God's work fulfilled on Earth, genuine love and care for the Body of Christ, unity of the Spirit, protection from false and misleading teaching, sincere guidance and necessary correction for personal transformation and ongoing growth and spiritual mature into the fullness of Christ.

Mission for Effective Journey

I started the journey with Jesus helping me to run the race with focus on the finishing line. Serving God or living for God is not an event, but it is a process that touches every part of our being. For this reason, on my journey I found that having a biblical concept of ministry is very important. Ministry is not activities we do for God when we feel that we are qualified. It is our wholehearted obedience to the revealed will of God, as we are being transformed daily into the likeness of Christ by the power of the Holy Spirit. That has been my life mission on this journey since the beginning.

This allows the process to be enjoyable. Because of my commitment to remain in the center of God's will, I don't strive for anything except simply obeying His voice. That is what I call true rest in the Lord leading to success and prosperity. But it won't always be obvious from a human standpoint. Conversely, when we're not in the center of God's will, even when we look successful, we fail.

Staying in the Center of His Will

For my 50th birthday I was in Nairobi, Kenya. As a child, since I was born and grew up in the countryside, I don't remember my parents celebrating my birthday. I don't have any birth records either. Therefore, my birthday has been just another day. However, on my 50th birthday something happened. I was in Nairobi, Kenya conducting a partner development leadership workshop for CI. After a long day of working with pastors, bishops and invited church leaders I went back to the Fairview Hotel. I prayed and organized my presentation for the next day and went to bed to get a good night rest for the following day workshop; however, I received a call from the front desk. A lady said, "I am sorry, sir, for disturbing you. You have guests who would like to see." I told her that since I am in bed already, I will see whoever it is at breakfast tomorrow morning. She responded, "It is urgent, and they would like for you to come to the reception." I dressed and went to meet them. It was some friends who found out that it was my birthday. They brought birthday cake to celebrate my 50th birthday. After they left, I went back to my room to sleep. I started reflecting on my birthday, and my relationship with my father. Even though my father never celebrated my birthday, he loved me and was proud of me. But celebrating birthdays was not part of the countryside culture.

I said to myself, *Now I have my heavenly Father who understands*. I left my bed and knelt before the Lord to ask my heavenly Father for birthday gifts. I said to the Lord, "My heavenly Father I would like to ask for two birthday gifts. The first one is whatever days you will give to live on Earth starting tonight, help me to stay in the center of your will!" The second gift is, "I would like you to go with me wherever you send me for ministry the remaining of my days." In other words, "I only want to go when and where you send me and confirm your manifested presence. Amen!"

After the three-day workshop, I went to Addis Ababa for another leadership training workshop. On my arrival Pastor Mesfin picked me up and went to the Hilton Hotel. We knelt to pray for the workshop and praised the Lord for what He had done in Nairobi. As we were praying, a word of prophecy came through Pastor Mesfin confirming my birthday requests. I didn't tell Pastor Mesfin about my birthday prayer, and he didn't know anything about it. I accepted my birthday gifts from my heavenly Father, finished my ministry and came home. I arrived in Colorado Springs on Saturday and went to church on Sunday morning. At that time Apostle Dutch Sheets was my pastor. In the middle of his preaching, he stopped and spoke with a voice of authority, "'Alemu Beeftu, you are my friend. I heard your prayers,' says the Lord." At that point, I lost it. I wept before the Lord and affirmed my covenant to stay in the center of His will the rest of my life. That has been my mission and focus since then.

Mission, Vision and Dream

Impact is the result of starting with God and walking with Him daily by being in His will, seeing and hearing Him. These three enabled me to define my mission, clarify my vision and affirm my dream. For an effective journey mission, vision and dreams are interdependent. Strong, effective life and ministry are built to advance God's Kingdom established on a proper sequence of these three elements, and the relationship between them.

A prophetic journey has a beginning and purpose. In the context of God's calling or divine assignment, my mission is the reason of my existence.

As we were discussing mission recently, one of my friends told me of a scene from the movie *2001: A Space Odyssey*. In this scene, astronauts wake up to discover the supercomputer that runs their spacecraft has actually killed some of their colleagues during an historic HAL, artificial intelligence attack. He explained his murderous behavior with a simple sentence: "The mission is too important to allow you to jeopardize it."

What a remarkable contrast between our Lord and this machine! God uses mission to establish me, to teach and develop us, into even greater disciples. God uses my life mission to help me answer the foundational question of prophetic destiny, *Who am I?* The answer to this question comes from knowing and answering, "Who are you, Lord, in my life?" Once I understood who God is in my life, I was able to accept who I am in Him. That helped me to establish my identity. For me the question of *Why am I here?* is all about defining my mission; the purpose of my existence. As I stated earlier in this book, that enabled me to understand the core of my mission, which has been *total obedience to the revealed will of God on my life journey.* Knowing and accepting God's will enables us to bear spiritual fruit that brings glory to the Father (John 15). That's why establishing my mission is the basis for everything. Having lasting impact is the result of this. A clear mission provides a strong foundation for success in every area of life, ministry and business. What is success? In this context, *success is reaching your prophetic destiny by accepting the call of God and faithfully obeying His purpose.*

In Kingdom life, obeying the purpose of God for one's life is the necessary step that follows accepting God's call. Success is far more than merely achieving a desired goal or completing the prophetic journey I have been on. It means exceeding calling, mission and purpose to release divine favor for a greater impact on my generation.

Mission is the key to measure the level of my submission to God's will. Submission to His will is to carry out the work of His kingdom and demands knowledge of His will. His will is completely consistent with His calling and mission for me. This pattern is demonstrated in the lives of the saints, both in the New and the Old Testament.

> Before I formed you in the womb I knew [and] approved of you [as My chosen instrument], and before you were born I separated and set you apart, consecrating you; [and] I appointed you as a prophet to the nations.
>
> Jeremiah 1:5 AMP

The basis of Jeremiah's success was not his skill, giftedness or maturity. It was his acceptance of God's purpose in his life. To live a life of submission, having a clear mission in life is necessary to embrace the call of God. It is similar in the life of Paul, the great apostle of the Lord Jesus Christ.

> But when God, who set me apart from birth and called me by his grace, was pleased to reveal his Son in me so that I might preach him among the Gentiles, I did not consult any man.
>
> Galatians 1:15-16

Like Jeremiah, Paul's basis of success was fully submitting his life in response to the issue of total obedience rather than describing his daily activities. "So then, King Agrippa, I was not disobedient to the vision from heaven" (Acts 26:19).

The Four Things Godly Mission Demands

Knowing God's Will

In turn, our mission should engage us in ways that maximize our impact and multiply our fruitfulness. Only then can I establish my mission in life, which leads us to live Kingdom principles for the glory of the King.

This is a fundamental issue for me. I recognized my call and established my mission at an early stage in my journey. That helped me to focus on serving God's purpose. God's purposes aren't meant to be vague. When Ananias brought Paul the news of God's calling on Paul to be an apostle, Ananias emphasized three things.

> The God of our fathers has chosen you to know his
> will and to see the Righteous One and to hear words
> from his mouth.
>
> Acts 22:14

First, Paul had to know God's will. The most important thing for leaders is to know the will of God, both for themselves and the people they lead in ministry, business, or any other endeavor. There is no substitute for the will of God to achieve Kingdom success and prosperity. Second, Paul needed a clear vision of Christ daily. When Christian leaders lose the vision of Christ, ministry becomes merely activity. The vision of Christ gives each leader direction and achievable, God-sized goals. Third, Paul had to hear the voice of the Lord. Hearing the voice of God is a source of encouragement in obeying the will of God.

Having God's Heart.

The knowledge of God's will is most effective in our lives when we have God's heart. God is far more interested in the condition of my heart than the quantity of my head knowledge.

The Lord called David, a simple shepherd turned into king, "A man after his heart." Yet, God also noted that Solomon, once the wisest man in the world, was not fully devoted to him. In comparing the two men 1 Kings 11:4 says, "His [Solomon's] heart was not fully devoted to the LORD his God, as the heart of David his father had been."

How can we secure the heart of God? If you are in covenant relationship with God, it's as simple as accepting His covenant promise. "I will give you a new heart and put a new spirit in you; I will remove from you your heart of stone and give you a heart of flesh" (Ezekiel 36:26).

What is the sign of God's heart in us? It is a sense of inner purity toward God and others. This leads to heartfelt demonstrations of compassion, forgiveness, righteousness, and love as you carry out

God's calling. God's heart in us will offer everythi: accomplish our mission with an undying love and true p and His purpose in our lives. When we have the hea desire or have a powerful longing to see Him.

When my son Ammanuel was young, I had an intense traveling schedule, and he wanted to come with his mom to pick me up at the airport. Since this was before the 9/11 attack on New York City, he asked my wife, Genet, if they could go to the gate to watch for my coming out. He would look very hard to spot me coming out, then run as fast as he could toward me. When I saw Ammanuel run toward me, I dropped whatever I was carrying and waited for him with opened hands. When he reached me instead of hugging me, he stretched his hands as a sign to pick him up. When I picked him up, he was content and happy. That is a sign of pure, loving heart.

Accomplishing God's purpose is far more than being busy for God. It is carrying out the agenda of the Kingdom through a living relationship with God, and that relationship demands a pure heart to carry it to its fullness. Jesus taught, "Blessed are the pure in heart, for they will see God" (Matthew 5:8). Your ability to keep a clear vision of Christ requires a pure heart.

Exercise the Mind of Christ

Much is written in the Word about the mind. One's heart is the fountain of life. In contrast, the mind directs the renewed mind. The mind that is not controlled by the Holy Spirit, sometimes called the *carnal mind*, is controlled by human desire. In contrast, the mind of God

)oth pure and all-knowing. The thoughts and ways of the Creator of the Universe are beyond our human understanding. That is why we need the mind of Christ, which can be ours as God renews our way of thinking (Romans 12:2).

A mind that is not renewed by the power of God's word can't do God's will. By function, the carnal mind, controlled by the human desire, works against God's purpose. "The sinful mind is hostile to God" (Romans 8:7).

Fulfilling the Holy Spirit's direction and the Word of God daily is the foundation to have the mind of Christ. When I have the mind of Christ, I think differently. I operate with God's value system. I don't want my daily actions controlled by my desires, ideas or emotion, but by the mind of Christ. This is why it is so crucial to have a mind renewed.

The Power of the Holy Spirit.

My best efforts alone will never accomplish Kingdom work. Divine work for the Kingdom agenda requires divine power from the Holy Spirit. The Lord declared this truth long ago by saying, "'Not by might nor by power, but by my Spirit,' says the LORD Almighty" (Zechariah 4:6).

The Holy Spirit is God. God, the Holy Spirit, is not about denomination. God is bigger than any denomination, any personal experience, or historical event we have read or seen.

Since I am committed to carry out the mission of the Kingdom, I come with an open mind to this point in the journey. I don't tell God what He can or can't do with me, but simply obey the Lord wholeheartedly.

The Lord Jesus Christ, who came to do the will of His Father, was totally dependent on the Holy Spirit to provide a pattern to follow. I utterly depend on the Holy Spirit, new birth; filling, leading, empowering, anointing, revelation of the Word and spiritual gifts to be fruit in the Kingdom work for the glory of the Father and King Jesus Christ.

As I have mentioned previously, everything has a beginning and purpose including the journey for prophetic destiny. Mission is the reason to exist in the context of God's calling or divine assignment to enjoy the King and the Kingdom blessings. "You prepare a table before me in the presence of my enemies. You anoint my head with oil; my cup overflows. Surely goodness and love will follow me all the days of my life, and I will dwell in the house of the LORD forever" (Psalm 23:5-6). This is the summary of Kingdom blessings.

CHAPTER 14

PROVISION FOR THE PROPHETIC DESTINY

If you are willing and obedient, you will eat the best from the land.

Isaiah 1:19

Vision

The Kingdom of God is all about godly vision. Since I met the Lord, my prayer has been to see His glory. I believe this is the passion or fire the Lord placed in heart. The burning desire I have to see His glory has protected me from wavering on my life journey. The New Testament Church started with visions and dreams. "'In the last days,' God says, 'I will pour out my Spirit on all people. Your sons and daughters will prophesy, your young men will see visions, your old men will dream dreams'" (Acts 2:17).

When we respond to the divine invitation to be His children, the Lord's will for us is to have open eyes, know the hope of our calling (mission), the riches of His glorious inheritance, and His incomparably great power. The Lord's desire is not only to see His greatness and understand His purpose for my life, but also to know the rich store He has. "He will be the sure foundation for your times, a rich store of salvation and wisdom and knowledge; the fear of the LORD is the key to this treasure" (Isaiah 33:6).

As I mentioned in a previous chapter, mission, vision and dream are connected on the journey of our prophetic destiny. I started with mission and committed to live for it. And then the Lord started giving me vision for my calling and future. One of the challenging things is that Kingdom vision doesn't come like a huge tree, but as a small seed with potential to become a big tree. It is very easy to overlook that small seed and keep looking for a tree. That is how the Lord taught me to be faithful in small things so that He can trust me with big things. My mission is based on my faith and trust in Him. My vision is based on the hope I have in the Lord.

Vision is my ability to see what is not yet at hand. In other words, to see a big tree in the seed I have been given. Vision enables me to envision, or see through a mental picture, what I don't observe with my physical eyes. Vision, in my life context, is the ability to see the future with all its potential and possibilities, and refuse to settle for anything less. It is inspiring to see or sense with an anticipation of what God has for me. Seeing what God sees for me and in me creates an excitement that results from the anticipation of what is coming. That helps me to get ready for what is coming instead of dwelling on the past. "Forget the former things; do not dwell on the past. See, I am doing a new thing!" (Isaiah 43;18-19). Vision leads to greater expectation and hope. Visionary leaders dress themselves in garments for what is coming rather than living in the past. We are to prepare for the future with new garments.

In relation to my mission, vision is the mental ability to see the possibilities and potential while pursuing the mission with excellence. My mission gives me general direction and purpose for living. My vision has provided me with determination and a clearer strategy for a step of faith. Thus, my mission and vision are interwoven.

From the day I accepted the Lord even without understanding vision, I had always been motivated to strive for what should be instead of being content with what is. That is why I had always been racing toward the goal. This is one of the reasons why this has been my favorite verse of scripture.

> Not that I have already obtained all this, or have already been made perfect, but I press on to take hold of that for which Christ Jesus took hold of me. Brothers, I do not consider myself yet to have taken hold of it. But one thing I do: Forgetting what is behind and straining toward what is ahead, I press on toward the goal to win the prize for which God has called me heavenward in Christ Jesus.
>
> Philippians 3:12-14

Vision is not denying the challenges of the present, it is rather focusing on what is coming to meet the present. In other words, I try to see the future without denying the reality of the present situation or circumstances. By looking forward, vision refuses to be limited by the present. God's interaction with Abram (Abraham), offers a powerful picture of vision. "The LORD said to Abram after Lot had parted from him, 'Lift up your eyes from where you are'" (Genesis 13:14).

Kingdom vision is to mobilize the people of God to use their gifts to serve others and glorify the Lord.

> Where there is no vision [no revelation of God and His word], the people are unrestrained; But happy and blessed is he who keeps the law [of God].
>
> Proverbs 29:18 AMP

In my opinion, a healthy or normal vision provides not only direction, but also steps of action to accomplish a mission and provide ongoing momentum and improvement. My vision has created a desire in my life to strive to be the best in what I have been given. It also helped me to identify my life core values. It is much like the prayer of Peter Marshall, a pastor in the mid-20th century who served as chaplain for the U.S. Senate: "Give to us clear vision that we may know where to stand and what to stand for—because unless we stand for something, we shall fall for anything."

The source of true vision is God. It is strengthening to see what God sees clearly while its value is to see the way God sees things. That is why the Apostle Paul said, "I was not disobedient to the vision from heaven" (Acts 26:19). Godly vision comes by having the heart of the Father, the mind of Christ, the anointing power and presence of the

Holy Spirit, and the revelation or true understanding of the Word of God, just like my mission.

Dream

Mission provides confidence and authority. Vision gives us a basis for the core values that form our goals or strategic direction, and the passion to excel through a process of ongoing improvement as we see things through God's eyes. Our dream enhances possibilities that enable us to achieve ever-greater results.

The root of the Hebrew word for *dream* means *to be made healthy*, or *to recover*. That root meaning still applies to dreams that produce images, thoughts and impressions. God uses dreams to guide us to the strength and health available by being obedient to His will. Dreaming is thinking with the renewed mind to overcome limitations. Dreams encourage us to reach the will of God, and carry out His purpose. Dreams push the boundaries for greater results because of God's power within us. Dreams help us to overcome not only external limitations, but also internal limitations and hindrances. Maturity in faith and in one's spiritual life actually encourages us to dream. Perhaps that was one of the reasons the Book of Acts declares: "Your old men will dream dreams" (Acts 2:17).

A dream is bigger than life. Having a dream means touching the coming generations. For me, a dream is going beyond the limitation of ability and resources to complete the calling God entrusted to me. Dreamers are very important for the expansion of the Kingdom of God. However, on my journey I have learned that dreamers face many challenges. From my personal experiences, the core challenges of a dream and a dreamer include the following.

Dream Killers

The enemy of the Kingdom of God doesn't like people who dream God's dreams. And particularly, individuals who dream with God. The story of Joseph paints a very clear picture. The premier opposition, usually, comes from close friends and family members. It comes in the form of hatred, jealousy and ridicule. That is what Joseph's brothers did to him. They made an effort to kill him to stop his dream.

In my life journey, I have faced very similar things, at different degrees, many times. The enemy tried to kill me through my father first. After my father, I faced radical, socialist students who tried their best to kill me. On my journey, even those who were very close to me in ministry came against me many times and different places because of jealously. A number of times I resigned from my positions because of the spirit of jealousy that came against me. One day while we were praying with a prophet, whom I trust very much, he saw a vision. At that time, I was working with an international organization. In his vision, he saw a person and described him perfectly. He asked me if I knew this person. I told him that I know him very well. He said, "I see this person wiping from a white board your report and try to write his own. He is very jealous, and he is trying to take all the credit for the work you do." That has been my life story.

Character Assassinators

The enemy tried to manipulate Joseph's brothers to kill the dreamer and destroy the dream. When that didn't work, the enemy changed his strategy and came back to destroy Joseph's character through Potiphar's wife by speaking a love language. She approached him using her love language to seduce him. She was sent to destroy his character and stop him from fulfilling his prophetic destiny.

I fully identify with Joseph's story, but I would not go into details of my personal experiences to protect others. However, I made a decision to follow my conviction in spite of what others say or do. I am a firm believer that effectiveness as a dreamer is proven through my ability to think with a sound mind, strong character and clear vision without dwelling on what others say or do.

As he thinks in his heart, so is he.

Proverbs 23:7 NKJV

Provision for Kingdom Vision

The three most important areas dreamers should protect themselves from are the spirit of jealousy that tries to kill dreams and dreamers. Deception misleads to disqualify and causes preoccupation with provision to carry out the dream.

In regard to provision there are two major camps. The *first* group is very sincere and God-fearing who would like to fulfill God's call by paying the price. The problem with this group is that as much as they love the Lord, they tend to see provision, resources or wealth as something to be avoided or tolerate at best. Doing the will of God with much suffering or financial lack is considered as righteousness and a special virtue. As a result, they are always preoccupied with finances. Even when they have resources, they operate with poverty and a scarcity mentality. They try their best to please God by staying poor or pretending to be poor. They lack the spirit of joy and generosity. They don't practice principles of giving and receiving. They limit giving to their individual tithing for their church's income. The principles of tithing, firstfruits and love offerings are forms of worship. They spend too much time in trying to protect and save money at the expense of obeying God by faith and rejoicing in His goodness.

On the other hand, there are those whose primary focus is getting money and becoming rich. The emphasis is not fulfilling God's calling and purpose, but to advance their own agenda. The goal is to get money and become wealthy individuals. They are driven by the love of money which is the root of every evil desire and action. They assume ownership, rather than managing God's resources for the Kingdom work. In many cases, they abuse and misuse the resources. They are controlled and driven by greed, and they worship money and fame. They don't pay attention to what Jesus said about Kingdom resources.

> No one can serve two masters; for either he will hate the one and love the other, or he will stand by and be devoted to the one and despise and be against the other. You cannot serve God and mammon (deceitful riches, money, possessions, or whatever is trusted in).
>
> Matthew 6:24 AMP

A balanced approach is needed very much. Provision for the vision and dream we are given comes from the Lord. The Lord has prepared the provision for every vision He has assigned to us. Provision is provided in advance to carry out the assignments. We see these principles.

Creation

God created everything that was needed before He created Adam and Eve, and He gave them responsibilities. Five days of creation were for them to enjoy. Their primary responsibility was to manage the provision for the glory of the Creator. The provision is there but for the Lord to release it to us, we should be in the right place and mature in our character to able to manage the provision and embrace our call fully.

Covenant promises

Through His covenant, the Lord promised Abraham and his descendants to bless them and make them a channel of His blessings to the nations. The requirements were:

Obeying His voice

Now it shall come to pass, if you diligently obey the voice of the LORD your God, to observe carefully all His commandments which I command you today, that the LORD your God will set you high above all nations of the earth. And all these blessings shall come upon you and overtake you, because you obey the voice of the LORD your God.

Deuteronomy 28:1-2 NKJ

Honoring Him by their firstfruits, tithing, and love gifts

Honor the LORD with your wealth, with the firstfruits of all your crops;then your barns will be filled to overflowing, and your vats will brim over with new wine.

Proverbs 3:9-10

Prophetic Declaration

Throughout the Old Testament, the Lord encouraged His people to return to Him and enjoy His blessings.

You will have plenty to eat, until you are full, and you will praise the name of the LORD your God, who has worked wonders for you; never again will my people be shamed.

Joel 2:26

If you are willing and obedient, you will eat the best from the land.

Isaiah 1:19

Kingdom Blessings

The Lord Jesus gave a summary of His kingdom blessing in one verse. "Seek first his kingdom and his righteousness, and all these things will be given to you as well" (Matthew 6:33). There is no stronger promise than this about provision for the vision of the Kingdom. The Lord's instruction is that we are not to look for the provision, but His kingdom and the right stand or relationship with our King first. That is what releases the blessings, or all the provision. Provision for Kingdom works is being released by connecting the heavens and Earth. "Your will be done on earth as it is in heaven." In other words, the heavenly blessings are already established. "Praise be to the God and Father of our Lord Jesus Christ, who has blessed us in the heavenly realms with every spiritual blessing in Christ" (Ephesians 1:3). My responsibility is to bring heavenly blessings through total obedience to His perfect will in order to release earthly blessings. That is what God has promised when He said, "All these things will be given to you as well." Or "All these blessings shall come upon you and overtake you."

Provision for the vision is already done. As visionary and dreamer, my responsibilities include:

- Walk in financial integrity with my best ability. That is managing God's resources properly.

- Make the Lord first in everything I do. That is, "Loving the Lord my God with all my heart and with all my soul and with all my mind and with all my strength" (Mark 12:30).

- Focus on pleasing God by walking in faith. That is obeying the Lord because of what He said, not because of what I have in my hands or in my bank account since it is impossible to please God without faith. To please and honor him, "We live by faith, not by sight" (2 Corinthians 5:7).

- Know and accept the Lord's timing. The journey of our prophetic destiny that leads into a true prosperity and lasting blessings only operates in the context of relationship, time and space. I make an effort to dwell in His presence daily and wait upon Him for provision from the vision. In my case, sometimes it takes a longer time for the provision to come. During that time, the Lord does His work in us to prepare. For some assignments, the Lord does a deep work in us and that takes time.

Seek the Blessings for Kingdom Expansion

Provision for the vision is to expand Kingdom work. When we seek resources for the Kingdom of God, our focus is on the hand of God, both to bless and empower us to work. The Lord honored that kind of prayer even in the Old Covenant. The prayer of Jabez is a very good example. "Jabez cried out to the God of Israel, 'Oh, that you would bless me and enlarge my territory! Let your hand be with me, and keep me from harm so that I will be free from pain.' And God granted his request" (1 Chronicles 4:10).

The House Is Yours!

I always try to keep in mind, provision is a means for the vision. Therefore, I live for the vision and trust the Lord for provision. He has been faithful all my ministry life. We have been living by faith since I left CI in 1999 to fulfill my calling. We have not lacked anything. The house we are living in now is the most recent testimony to the goodness of the Lord. In 2015, we felt strongly the need to move from the house we purchased when we moved from Colorado to Texas. Though we liked the house and the neighborhood, driving from Prosper on regular basis to the Gospel of Glory office in Denton, the Dallas/Fort Worth airport and Emerging Glory Center in Richardson became too much. Yearly we averaged 55,000 miles in driving. We started looking for a home, by faith. Since we didn't have consistent pay stubs from an employer to show the lenders, we didn't know if the bank would qualify us. We put our home on the market with plans to move into an apartment. But the Lord said, "I have built for you, a house of glory." At almost the last minute, we found a house I liked before we closed on our home in Prosper. But we faced major problems. The first problem was the price of the house I liked. The second problem was we had only four days to close on our home and move out. The third problem was to become qualified by a lender.

However, in spite of all these challenges, I felt strongly to show the house to Genet on Sunday, even thought we were scheduled to close the sale on our home on Wednesday. She believed that the price would be out of our reach, and it would not work. I said to her, "But do you like the house?" She said, "I love the house, the location and the neighborhood." I took her back on Monday to look at the house one more time during daylight. In the meantime, I asked the banker I had worked with before, "In an ideal situation what would he qualify us for. He said, "Off the record if everything is perfect, I can qualify you for $_____this amount." I said, "Thank you!" and left his office.

On Monday, after we looked at the house again, I told the salesperson that I am ready to make an offer on one condition. He asked me what the condition was. I told him that if you promise that you will not be offended by my offer, I will make an offer. He said, "Go ahead." I started by telling him how beautiful the house is, who we are and what we do. I said, "The offer I'm going to make doesn't reflect the value of your house, but the basis for my offer would be what I think a bank would qualify us for, under the best scenario." I made an offer that was less by $130,000 from the asking price. He was shocked and speechless. He sat back and said, "Don't even think about it. I wouldn't mention this to the builder." Then, I said to him, "I disagree with you. It is your obligation to tell him, so he knows my offer. Let him make his own decision." We left his office and started driving to go home and continued packing to move into an apartment.

After we drove for about five minutes, my mobile phone rang. It was the same person. He said, "For a very strange reason, the builder would like to meet with you, if you can come back. He would be here in about 10 or 15 minutes." I said, "Okay, we will turn around and come back." When we came back, the builder was already there. He greeted us very warmly and opened the house we were interested in buying. He said, "My back is hurting. Is it okay if I sit on the counter?" We told him, "Sure, it is your home, and you are the builder." After he sat down, he said, "I don't want to talk about the house. Tell me about you. Who are you guys?" We shared with him about who we are, our journey and our present ministry. When he heard about my travel schedule, he asked me if I travel to dangerous places. I told him in about two weeks where I would be. He said, "I will pray for you." He asked, "Tell me how you two met?" Genet commented, "Do you have time to hear our story?" He said, "Yes, I would love to hear your story." We shared with him, and he heard us while fighting back his tears.

After we finished sharing, he said, "I don't meet with the buyers of my homes, and you guys are the first couple I have ever met with. When I heard your names, I had this urge to meet with you."

He said, "I just started building small homes in Argyle, Texas. In fact, in about four months, the first home will be ready for move in. For the price, you offered, I can sell that house to you and pay for your apartment." I said to him, "Thank you so much for meeting with us and the offer. But that would be too far from the office, and we will wait upon the Lord and see what His has for us." As we were leaving, Genet stretched her hand to give him a handshake. He said, "I want a hug," and gave us big hugs. He said, "Don't worry about the house. Let me meditate on it. I will call you tomorrow." We left. The next day, on Tuesday morning, he called me at 8:30 a.m. He asked if I felt okay. I told him that I felt very good. He said, "I didn't sleep. I was thinking about you guys all night. Does Genet still like the house? Do you still believe the house is yours?" I said, "Here is Genet; talk to her?" She told him that she loved the house. He said, "The house is yours for the offer you made, and I will tell my staff this morning. I will prepare paperwork, and you should come to my office tomorrow after you close on your house and sign it to start the process." He also said, "You can move your stuff into the garage, and that way you don't have to move twice." Genet started running around in the house praising the Lord.

Two weeks before, Chuck had asked us about the progress on the houses. We told him that in two weeks we will close on our home and move into an apartment for a while. He told Genet to ask Brian to make a hotel reservation for transition time. Genet told him that since we will move straight to an apartment, we won't need a hotel room. He said, "Just in case, tell him anyways."

After we closed on the house, we moved our stuff into the new home's garage, but we didn't have place to stay. Genet called Brian. Brian called back and said, "I made a reservation for you at Marriot Court in Denton for two weeks." The process took two weeks to close on the new house, which was a miracle in itself. We moved into our new home for a two-week stay. The hotel reservation was right on the exact date. It was amazing! The day we moved out from the hotel, we went to pay for the hotel, but it was already paid. What an awesome God!

Since we moved into this new home, we have been hosting Kingdom people continuously. It has been almost like bed and breakfast place. We have been blessed very much.

CHAPTER 15

ENVISIONING THE FUTURE

The LORD said to Abram after Lot had parted from him, "Lift up your eyes from where you are and look north and south, east and west."

Genesis 13:14

To finish well, you need a starting point. The starting point provides solid ground for the process to be successful. What is your starting point? Where are you? Start from where you are! Your life journey from this day forward isn't for the sake of the past, but for the future. For some, the present place is one step in a series of steps already taken for the future. For others, the present place is a place of completely starting over. For me, the starting point was my small countryside in a village call Maru.

I didn't start the journey of my prophetic destiny with a clear understanding of what the future holds, but moved forward. Please understand, I did not say my starting point had to be in the context of success. In fact, very few begin that way. The journey of our prophetic destiny is based on a desire to see what is next in order to envision the future from where I am. When the Lord took Abram on his journey, all the Lord said to him was, "Go for yourself [for your own advantage] away from your country, from your relatives and your father's house, to the land that I will show you" (Genesis 12:1 AMP, emphasis added).

"Go" is a command. The Lord took responsibility to show him the land, or a country he didn't know. Therefore, our journey has been moving from the known to the unknown by trusting the Lord and envisioning the future. In my case, envisioning the future is creating hope. In the village where I grew up, the most expensive commodity was future hope. If you are able to hope, you can envision the possibilities. When I started feeling what could happen or was possible, I was not able to look back. The more my desire for the past experiences diminished, my future became brighter. The unknown future became more attractive than what I had experienced in the past. My vision for the future became the driving force. It created in me a sense of direction with a greater hope and anticipation.

The Lord has confirmed my calling to be both like David and Abraham. It is like the David calling in two aspects: serving His purpose and preparing the emerging generation to be the arm of God. Like the Abraham calling to obey him by faith and to be a father for my generation. The Lord has established this aspect of my calling by many prophets.

The most recent affirmation of my calling was given by Barbara Wentroble.

"I just felt the spirit of the Lord say I've called you even as I have called Abraham, and I called Abraham to come out from where he was because I was going to cause him to be a father to nations. God says son I've called you out from where you were so that I could enlarge your capacity, and I could enlarge your influence. I say I am going to use you as a father to nations; not one nation, but many nations of the world. I will say even the heart of a father that's on the inside of you will break the fatherless spirit that is in those nations for God said it is the fatherless nation that leads to corruption and perversion and all of those evils of the world. God said you're going to lose the healing balm of the Father that shall go in and shall restore the hearts of the fathers to the children and the children to the fathers. I say a father to the nations of the world that will break the fatherless spirit and see restoration and healing come. I say even as you do that, you watch the statistics of those nations for I say even the criminal records will go down. I say even the alcohol and the drug abuse; watch it as it plummets says the Lord. I say where they have tried to fill their hearts with the things of this world, I say you shall fill them with the heart of the Father and the fatherless spirit shall be broken off of that generation. They shall rise up in this hour says the Lord. They shall rise up and they shall turn their hearts toward the Lord, and I say restoration and reformation will come into those places where you go."

On our journey one of the things is that even after we discovered God's will and settled on our prophetic destiny, the Lord would like to show us more. Again, Abram is a very good example for this. Abram brought with him Lot, his brother's son.

> The LORD said to Abram after Lot had parted from him, "Lift up your eyes from where you are and look north and south, east and west."
>
> Genesis 13:14

When we are in our place, the Lord would like for us to let go whatever we brought with us into our promise land, before He shows us the larger picture and vision. The name Lot in the Hebrew means a covering or veil. When a veil is removed, the Lord asks us to lift up our eyes and see what he has for us. When we see it, we can walk into it. The covering or veil comes off. We can build an altar of worship.

Everybody has a history and background. Your experience is the basis for starting. Without true desire or genuine passion, it is hard to start and stay on course. To stay on the course and envision the future, we must get rid of the past.

When we catch not only the hope of the future but passion for our prophetic destiny, nothing is able to stop us. I know. I'm living proof of God's grace. Starting points of almost any kind can be used to live a life for His glory and with His blessing. That is, if you have a burning desire to run the race of life with purpose and goal in mind.

The journey is like the starting point of a river. When it starts flowing, it doesn't stop, and we don't see the end of it or the last drop of that water.

Because of the passion I have been carrying with me about the next generation, I am always looking for a way to increase my involvement. We moved from Colorado Springs to the North Texas area to increase the impact on emerging young leaders. However, we didn't plan to start a local church in this area. But the Lord started giving us signs about an equipping and training center. The first signal came from Apostle Chuck Pierce at our first Gospel of Glory annual glory gathering.

Word by Apostle Chuck Pierce, November 19, 2910.

While we were worshipping, I heard the Lord say,

"Every tribe and every tongue." He kept saying it over and over, "Every tribe and every tongue." So, I kept asking the Lord, "What are You saying to us?" And I feel like what He's trying to do is get beyond our normal form of worship that we're in.

"Today is going to be several things. This will be an ending and a beginning for us, each one of us here. The second thing it's going to be, it's going to be the beginning of something new."

After this word, the Lord started confirming His plan. We started a quarterly meeting called Glory Gathering for every tongue and every tribe. It was powerful. At the last gathering we had – while I was speaking on the glory of God fire – local fire fighters came to put off fire. They said they saw smoke on the building and came to put out fire. They couldn't find any fire, of course, except the fire of His glory.

In the meantime, a dear brother came to minister in one of the churches in Oklahoma. We went to see him, and we joined him in ministering Sunday morning and drove together to our home. He had been asleep sitting in the front passenger seat. As I drove into our driveway, he woke up as soon as I stopped and said, "I heard the Lord saying you have six months to come up with strategy to start multi-cultural, multi-language, multi-ethnic, and multi-generational fellowship."

After that we accepted the mandate and started a Bible study group. In 2014, we established Emerging Glory Center (EGC) as an expansion of the vision of our prophetic destiny.

1. **Mission**

   Prepare the Body of Christ to restore His glory, host His presence and demonstrate the power of the Gospel.

2. **Vision**

   Equipping, modelling and sending out leaders with new vision to disciple nations and impact society at large.

3. **Goal**

   Establish the ministry of Shiloh, Siloam and Zion, in order

to move the Body of Christ from ordinary Christian life to extraordinary life and relationship with God so they would keep the centrality of Christ by **living, loving and serving** His purpose. Shiloh is a place of an altar of worship & revelation. Siloam is a place of sending with a new vision; impartation, activation and commissioning. Zion is a place of His dwelling presence.

Prepare and ordain fivefold ministry leaders

1. **Apostle:** Provides overall strategic leadership, direction and covering.
2. **Prophet:** Provides clear vision for long and short term strategic planning.
3. **Evangelist:** Reaches out to the lost and society at large with the good news of the Gospel of salvation.
4. **Pastor:** Provides care and guidance for the saints by meeting their needs in the context of their reality.
5. **Teacher:** Equips the saints for the work of the ministry.

Build Kingdom movement

Reach a multi-cultural, multi-language, multi-ethnic, and multi-generational fellowship for worship, celebration, and discipleship. Demonstration of the power of the Gospel to shape an evangelistic outreach in the greater Dallas area, the USA and around the world.

Enhance local church mission and vision

- Fulfill the biblical mandate of bringing the Kingdom of God to Earth.
  Worship God in spirit and truth (John 4:24).

- Witness: Fulfill the Great Commission by evangelizing nations (Matthew 28:19-21).

- Work of ministry. Equip the saints (Ephesians 4:12-13).

- Work of mercy. Care for the poor, respond to human needs (Galatians 2:10). World outreach. Be the light of the world (Matthew 5:14).

Strategy

- Establish center for teaching, training, equipping and mobilizing Kingdom workers.

- Establish a biblical government to equip and send to invade, occupy and transform by understanding, accepting and living by the government the Lord mandated for His church (1 Corinthians 12:28).

- Support ministry of mobilizing armies, equipping and empowering the saints, providing spiritual covering for correction and guidance.

- Build accountability network(s) for correcting history and make history shaping the future for lasting transformation.

Hence, EGC is a training center where God's altar is kept pure.

Worship fire is alive for His presence to dwell, where the revelation of His Word can be released, where His light will shine, and where the power of the Gospel is demonstrated. The focus is to plant churches and mentor church leaders to establish divine order in local churches through the fivefold ministry, to advance the Kingdom and impact generations.

Multi-Cultural Fellowship

Build a multi-cultural, multi-language, multi-ethnic, and multi-generational fellowship for worship, celebration, and discipleship. Establish and model a fivefold ministry leadership to reach the lost, disciple the saints, and equip and send out leaders with new vision to disciple nations and impact society at large.

Reach Ethiopians and Eritreans

Build a new church movement throughout the United States and plant new churches that will serve as a model of biblical government and fivefold leadership, with true worship and demonstration of the power of the Gospel to shape evangelistic outreach for this target group.

Our long-term call is to **shape evangelistic outreach in both the USA and worldwide.** The Word of the Lord is that we will usher in the light of His glory to the people who don't know His glory.

Therefore, EGC is a movement to mobilize, equip and empower Kingdom workers. Spiritual covering for guidance for emerging leaders who would invade, occupy and transform by understanding, accepting and living by the government the Lord has in place for His church (1 Corinthians 12:28).

CONCLUSION

They overcame him by the blood of the Lamb and by
the word of their testimony.

Revelation 12:11

Glory to God in the Highest! Thank You for your faithfulness! As I write this book and read it, again and again, the faithfulness of God and His goodness are forever imprinted on my heart and soul. This book is about the faithfulness of God as it relates to my life journey. I used my personal testimony to give glory to God and highlight the importance of a prophetic destiny that God has planned and called for each person. He desires for us to live an abundant life and with maximum impact on their spheres of influence. Such a Christian journey has some identifiable stages once we hear and respond to the call of God for an eternal relationship. God's call, which gives us breakout for breakthrough, includes "From," "To" and "For."

- **From**

  God's call is to move us from the past to prepare us for our future. I call this breakout for breakthrough as we obtain lasting freedom in Christ through the forgiveness sin. That is becoming a new creation by accepting the Lord Jesus Christ as personal Lord and Savior by repenting from our sins. We do this by admitting that we are sinners, and we need Jesus Christ the Savior who died for us, was buried, and rose from the dead. Through prayer, you are able to invite Jesus into your heart to become your personal Lord and Savior. He is the God who redeems. He restores relationship with each and every person who establishes covenant with Him. His promises are great! No matter where we are at in life, we start with the first step, accepting God as Lord of our life. When we have trust in Him, our life is being transformed – the old yoke is broken, sin lost it power – previous moral and spiritual condition are changed. "Therefore, if anyone is in Christ, he is a new creation; the old has gone, the new has come!" (2 Corinthians 5:17). Now we can forget the past and focus on the new hope with a greater anticipation and hope for the future. Because of that hope, we have a courage to start a new journey of life with a renewed vision and purpose in life.

- **To**

God calls us to relationship with Him by becoming His child. When we remember God's faithfulness, we also remember His everlasting covenant. When we accept Jesus Christ as our personal Savior, we enter into a covenant with God. Holy Spirit in us provides an ongoing living relationship with our Creator. God calls us to Himself to live with Him as his children calling Him "Abba Father." How great is that? It is a challenge to comprehend this supernatural relationship. It is supernatural! Beyond our comprehension, but we learn to trust in this relationship. This becomes our reality daily, and this prepared us for our His will. "Jesus went up on a mountainside and called to him those he wanted, and they came to him" (Mark 3:13). Through this relationship we understand His heart and His purpose. That gives clearer direction for a long-term journey of life. In this process, we mature in our character and develop a stronger biblical worldview and lasting core values of starting right, walking straight and finishing well as a sent one with a sense of accountability. This process is important as we learn how to trust God. In stage one "From," we learn to trust. At this stage, we learn to trust Him and run to see Him. On the journey of life if we don't know how to run to Him and stay close, we would not have power to run for Him to finish well.

- **For**

God calls us to send us to do His work on Earth which is our prophetic destiny. It is what we are created for. We start our life journey by accepting and embracing God's plan and purpose by coming to Him and dwelling in His presence. Now we can start our own journey of prophetic destiny since we have a breakout from the old, we can focus on the breakthrough. The Holy Spirit will enable you to experience breakthrough in our life. That is what I am referring to as "breakthrough" in the title of this book. Breakthrough is the result of following God's leading to be empowered to be His witness on earth.

> He appointed twelve—designating them apostles—that they might be with him and that he might send them out to preach and to have authority to drive out demons.
>
> Mark 3:14-15

What you have read in this book is a testimony with biblical principles that shows God's faithfulness of a journey of prophetic destiny by breakout from things that hold us back from fulfilling God's purpose and experience breakthrough to reach our destination responding to the call of the Gospel, "Follow me." We can only reach the destination God created, saved and anointed us for by following the One who is the way, the truth and the life since it is written.

> One who breaks open the way will go up before them; they will break through the gate and go out. Their king will pass through before them, the LORD at their head.
>
> Micah 2:13

For some the question is: *Why is it essential to give verbal testimony to glorify God, as directed by Revelation 12:11?* When we testify, we are verbally saying, "God, you are able to repeat your power in my life. You are the Creator of the Universe. You have the power to restore. I witnessed your power in the past. I know you can do it again. Do it again, Lord."

When you read my testimony, you may think,

> That is for other people but not for me. I have made such a big mess of my life; I can't receive the fulness of God's blessings. I don't know where to start. I am not worthy. I am not good enough.

But remember, our God is supernatural.

Genet, my wonderful wife, my beautiful daughter, Keah Alemu Beeftu, and incredible son, Ammanuel Alemu Beeftu are a testimony to God's goodness and faithfulness as I have traveled to over 50 nations. They have been alongside me everywhere I go, even though they are not able to travel with me everywhere physically. Since I accepted my prophetic destiny to declare His glory to the nations, I always pray for nations. Previously I had a big world map in my prayer room, and now I have one in my office. Every morning I look at that map and pray over the nations as the Holy Spirit leads me. After our children were born, we decided to involve them in our calling to the nations. We made sure this is not just Genet and Alemu's ministry but our ministry as a family. Therefore, we used the same map to involve our two children. Every time I received an invitation to go to another country to minister, during our family devotions we asked our children to find the location of the city and country. After that until the day of my travel, we prayed for that city and country by pointing out at it on the map. The night before my travel, they lay their hands on me and send me as a representative for them in doing the work of God. While I am gone, I give them a report about what the Lord doing. Upon returning home, I give them a report, and we pray together and praise the Lord. That way they stay fully involved in the international ministry. I am so thankful to the Lord for their commitment to the Lord and determination to make a difference in their prophetic generation. For us, the journey of prophetic destiny is a family journey as much as individual. All are committed. Words cannot express my love for them and my gratitude to the Lord for His goodness on this journey for me and my family.

My encouragement to you is that you share verbally your personal testimony. Give God the glory for your life. Continually remember your everlasting covenant with God, the Creator of the Universe. There is no one like you. You are created in His image. You have a prophetic journey to move from ordinary lifestyle into an extraordinary relationship with the Lord Jesus Christ. Our God is the Living God.

Alemu Beeftu
Gospel of Glory
Denton, Texas

ABOUT THE AUTHOR

Dr. Alemu Beeftu, founder and president of Gospel of Glory, has a heart for training pastors, businessmen and politicians with a goal of building national leadership infrastructures. Dr. Beeftu presently concentrates on transformational leaders of various ages in more than 54 countries who have the calling, gifting and character to foster sustainable societal change for the kingdom of God.

Beeftu grew up on an isolated farm in the Ethiopian countryside. At age 12 his desire to read caused him to run away to a missionary school, where he learned to read and write—and find a Savior. When a Communist government brought persecution on the Ethiopian church in the late 1970s, Beeftu, by then a recognized evangelist and youth leader, made his way to the United States.

Beeftu earned a BA from Biola University and master's and doctoral degrees in Curriculum Design and Community Development from Michigan State University. More than 30 years of practice in these and related fields have made Dr. Beeftu an accomplished and sought-after leadership trainer. He, also, continues to provide leadership worldwide for the Body of Christ.

Dr. Beeftu's most recently authored books include: *Divine Pattern For the Fullness of His Glory, God's Questions, Restoration for Lasting Transformation, Igniting Leaders for Kingdom Impact, Wrestling for Your Prophetic Destiny, Put Your Heart Above Your Head, Restoring the Altar For*

Fresh Fire, Leadership Journey, Spiritual Accountability, and *Leading for Kingdom Impact, Determination to Make a Difference, and others.*

Dr. Beeftu and his wife, Genet, make their home in Highland Village, Texas with their children Keah and Amman.

To obtain more information about Dr. Beeftu and how to invite him to speak to your organization go to www.Goglory.org.

www.goglory.org
Email: gog@goglory.org
Mailing address
P.O.Box 1719
Lake Dallas, TX 75065

Made in the
USA
Columbia, SC